LEARN

A 5-Step Framework for Designing Culturally Meaningful Practices

Dwayne D. Williams, PhD

THE LEARN FRAMEWORK FOR PRACTICE

I feel that I can run culturally responsive sessions now and have enough of an understanding and methods to implement the work, but I wish I was doing this sooner.

—PhD Research Participant

A Dwayne D. Williams Publication

Cover design: Nabin Karna

Editor: Sam Wright

Books by Dr. Williams

The Hero's Journey: How Seven School-Based Practitioners Learned to Design Culturally Meaningful Activities—and How You Can Too!

ISBN: 979-8-9873114-1-7

Redesign: An SEL Toolkit to Designing Culturally Sustaining and Antiracist Practices

ISBN: 978-0-9847157-2-5

Like Music to My Ears: A Hip-Hop Approach to Addressing Social and Emotional Learning and Trauma in Schools

ISBN: 978-0-9847157-5-6

An RTI Guide to Improving the Performance of African American Students

ISBN: 978-1483319735

Human Behavior from a Spiritual Perspective: Spiritual Development Begins in Your Mind

Book 1—ISBN: 978-0984715794

Book 2—ISBN: 978-0984715787

Visit Begin with Their Culture Bookstore to View Additional Resources at the Website Below

Contact Dr. Williams at

Email: dwayne@tier1education.com

Website: www.tier1education.com

Twitter: @dwaynedwilliams

Facebook: www.facebook.com/Tier1services

LinkedIn: @dwaynedwilliams

Instagram: @dwaynedwilliamsphd

TikTok: @DwayneDWilliamsPhD

YouTube: @Dwayne D. Williams

Podcast—*The Begin With Their Culture Podcast: Unboxing Culturally Meaningful Teaching*

Facebook Private Group—*Redesign: An SEL Toolkit for Designing Culturally Meaningful Practices*

The LEARN Academy: See our website for more information: https://tier1education.com

What Educators Are Saying

This book packs a punch while taking very little time to read. It provides history to illustrative definitions of sometimes confusing terms and real-life examples for additional clarity. The short exercises allow the reader to stay engaged and reflect on their beliefs throughout the chapters. The author's expertise and passion for culturally meaningful work shines through every page. His deep-dive into this work teaches the most novice educator how to build a culturally meaningful practice from the ground up! It's a must-read for anyone who wants to connect to students!

—Dr. Tiffany Gholson, K-12 Administrator

This book covers EVERYTHING you need to know to be able to design culturally meaningful activities in your classroom! Dr. Williams outlines how to be a culturally responsive educator in a thorough and easy to understand fashion. He provides practical tools, gives specific examples, and guides you from start to finish on your journey. I went from not knowing how to design culturally responsive groups to independently running my own groups. I now coach staff members in my building after going through his training and reading this book. This book outlines all of his research and puts it together in an easy-to-understand format. I go back to this book when I feel stuck and need to re-examine my practices. I wish I had this book many years ago!

—Kate Kokenes, K-12 Social Worker

Dr. Williams does an incredible job of guiding the reader through a real process. The space he gives to engage in meaningful reflection encourages the reader along a journey that will allow them to create curriculum, sessions, and meetings that will engage their students. Engaging with his LEARN framework will make the reader a better and more impactful educator. I feel strongly that every teacher training program should have this as a required text!

—Katie Khami, K-12 High School Counselor

I am an educator that works with Dr. Williams. I have sought out his expertise to help make my U.S. History curriculum more culturally responsive. Many strategies he presents in this book I have implemented into lessons have helped me bond with my students of all backgrounds. Dr. Williams's insights have helped me grow as a mature educator. They also have helped my students like U.S. History.

—Emily Polacek, K-12 Teacher

Dr. Williams book, LEARN: A 5 Step Framework for Designing Culturally Meaningful Practices, is filled with a feeling of honest reflection from teachers and Dr. Williams himself. In addition, there is a consistent vibe that we are in this together. This book brings accessibility to Culturally Meaningful Practices that make up Culturally Responsive Education. Readers are pushed with love to learn the history of culturally responsive education, understand the theories of Ladson-Billings, Gay, and Paris, challenge/problematize their practices, and explore their cultural values/practices compared to their culturally diverse students. In turn, teachers are able to recognize historical and cultural practices that have limited the untapped and abundant skill-sets of black, brown, and other culturally neglected groups. LEARN is an action-oriented piece that encourages teacher agency and empowerment. It emphasizes tools, methods, values, and reflection techniques that can be used right away. Most importantly, LEARN brings student voice to the forefront, energizing student participation in the development and implementation of their education. Teachers using this book will benefit from gained historic, theoretical, and introspective knowledge, along with actionable practices and a clear view on how community collaboration with peers and students can lead to essential vulnerability, growth, and a chance to create change.

—Matt Kahler, K-12 Teacher

Contents

A Note to the Reader

Dear Reader:

Since 2011, I have successfully co-designed culturally responsive practices with students and coached educators on how to design culturally meaningful activities. My knowledge of culturally responsive education (CRE) and design has increased since 2011. I now create culturally responsive practices intentionally, using specific frameworks. This book introduces *The LEARN Framework for Practice* as one of many tools to design culturally meaningful activities. In this book, I share over 16 years of knowledge on developing practical, culturally meaningful strategies and over ten years of knowledge coaching educators on equity principles. In addition, I provide four useful tools that teachers and administrators who participated in my PhD research study found helpful for designing culturally meaningful activities.

When I train educators on my work, they often say, "Dwayne, I love your approach to culturally responsive teaching. My students would love this process!" They then say, "But how do I do it?" This book shows you how to do it. I will resolve two common problems thousands of educators experience concerning culturally responsive teaching. These two problems prevent practitioners from applying culturally responsive teaching principles in the classroom and, thus, prevent them from designing equitable practices.

These problems include (1) lacking the basic knowledge of culturally responsive teaching and (2) lacking knowledge of how to design culturally responsive practices. The first problem leads to the second: If practitioners lack knowledge of culturally responsive teaching—i.e., definitions, principles, and frameworks—they will experience many barriers preventing them from designing culturally meaningful activities intentionally and purposefully.

It is possible to design effective instructional practices without knowing culturally responsive theories, principles, and frameworks. However, it is impossible to design culturally responsive activities if you do not know culturally responsive theories, principles, and frameworks. At least you cannot do it *intentionally* and *purposefully* based on CRE scholarship.

You cannot do it intentionally because culturally responsive teaching is the application of CRE scholarship. It is the practice of placing the *cultural values, community practices,* and *lived experiences* of students at the center of instruction. It is also the practice of critiquing and challenging the status quo and teaching students how to do it. Therefore, culturally responsive frameworks comprise principles that inform us on what to focus on as we design culturally meaningful practices.

As I mentioned earlier, educators I have coached on culturally responsive teaching have described two common challenges with CRE. These include lacking knowledge of culturally responsive teaching and lacking knowledge of how to design culturally responsive practices. I wrote this book to address these two problems. By the end of this book, you will know what culturally responsive teaching is and what it is not. You will have knowledge of and access to *The 5-Step LEARN Framework for Practice,* a framework designed by and for practitioners to guide you as you prepare culturally meaningful practices. Practitioners and I co-designed and then used this framework in my PhD research study to design culturally meaningful practices. In this book, I introduce *The LEARN Framework* so you can develop culturally meaningful and equitable activities as practitioners did within my research.

Acknowledgements

I dedicate this book to the seven educators in my PhD research study. Thank you for your willingness to challenge yourselves and each other during the 7-week training. You all shared things during the training I never considered concerning culturally meaningful teaching. You all have advanced my knowledge in significant ways about designing culturally meaningful activities.

Special shoutout to Sasha (pseudonym), who organized my professional development training materials and created the acronym *LEAR*. Days later, I included the letter *N*, to create *The LEARN Framework for Practice*. Words cannot express how much I appreciate your contribution to this work. Thank you. To all seven practitioners—this one is for y'all.

In solidarity,
Dwayne D. Williams, PhD

About the Author

Dwayne D. Williams, PhD, is a school psychologist, interventionist, and equity coach. As an equity coach, Dr. Williams helps organizations design and redesign educational practices. Specifically, he helps teams create culturally meaningful, inclusive, and equitable programming that integrates instruction with students' cultural assets and lived experiences. Additionally, he provides training to school districts on how to design problem-solving models, multi-tiered supports, restorative practices, social and emotional learning, and trauma-informed groups—all from a culturally meaningful lens.

Dr. Williams is the CEO of the consulting firm *Begin with Their Culture*, an organization that helps districts redesign educational practices in ways that pair issues of race, culture, and equity with instruction. He is the author of the book *An RTI Guide to Improving Performance of African American Students.* He has used his curriculum, *Like Music to My Ears: A Hip-Hop Approach to Addressing Social and Emotional Learning and Trauma in Schools,* with hundreds of students, and he coaches practitioners through designing activities that integrate SEL, cognitive-behavioral principles, and hip-hop cultural elements as methods of employing culturally meaningful practices for students who embrace the arts.

Dr. Williams earned his PhD from the University of Illinois at Chicago (UIC), where he studied curriculum and instruction. His scholarship focuses on redesigning educational programming in ways that consider the cultural assets and lived experiences of culturally diverse learners. Dr. Williams lived in housing projects as a child in Springfield, Illinois, and often speaks on the need to connect with students, parents, and community leaders from underrepresented backgrounds to improve educational conditions for underrepresented groups.

Dr. Williams is married to Toni Williams, and together they have two children: Dwayne D. Williams II and Noni D. Williams.

Book Overview

SECTION 1—Learners Take Your Mark: *Understanding Teacher Agency and Tool Use*

I divided this book into four sections. *Section 1* lays the book's foundation by introducing two critical concepts related to culturally responsive teaching: (1) teacher agency and (2) mediational tools. Culturally responsive teaching requires that we involve ourselves in learning about culturally responsive principles and employing specific tools to design culturally responsive practices. In addition to highlighting agency and tools, Section 1 sheds light on my PhD research study, which inspired this book. From this section, you will learn that teacher agency and tool-use are the heart and soul of culturally responsive teaching.

Chapter 1, *Teacher Agency and Mediational Tools*, orients you to the importance of agency and tool use when designing culturally responsive practices. In this chapter, I define teacher agency and mediational tools, and I discuss why culturally responsive teaching requires agency and tool use. I discuss why it is impossible to design culturally responsive practices intentionally and purposefully without agency and tool use.

Chapter 2, *In the Beginning was . . . the Problem*, discusses the importance of identifying problems that prevent us from designing culturally responsive practices and employing tools to transform those problems. You will learn that culturally responsive teaching is much more than simply implementing technical, quick-tip solutions; it is identifying and transforming problems that prevent us from designing culturally responsive practices. Chapter 2 highlights five categories of problems that practitioners experienced during my research study that prevented them from designing culturally responsive practices. It emphasizes the importance of agency and tool use when transforming problems.

SECTION 2—Get Set:
Understanding Frameworks

Section 2 addresses the importance of frameworks in designing culturally responsive practices. Culturally responsive teaching employs frameworks in the classroom based on goals and objectives. During my research study, practitioners commented that they had never been trained in applying frameworks in the classroom and lacked knowledge of culturally responsive principles. In addition, I have trained thousands of educators on culturally responsive teaching, and like practitioners in my research study, in-service and pre-service teachers I have coached were unfamiliar with culturally responsive frameworks. Practitioners in my study were able to design culturally meaningful practices *after* learning about culturally meaningful frameworks. From this section, you will learn three frameworks you can use as guides when unpacking culturally responsive teaching and designing culturally meaningful activities.

Chapter 3, *The Meaning is in the Framework*, sheds light on the importance of framework names. In this chapter, I show that names and principles give meaning to frameworks. From this perspective, culturally *relevant*, culturally *responsive*, and culturally *sustaining* practices have a specific meaning based on the name of the framework and the principles that comprise it. Content from this chapter reveals the significance of frameworks when designing culturally meaningful practices.

Chapter 4, *The Historical Development of The LEARN Framework*, addresses how the *LEARN Framework* originated. The framework is rooted in research and practice. Specifically, it is grounded in years of practice as an interventionist and school psychologist, and its five core principles (*LEARN*–learn, examine, adopt/adapt, reflect, and negotiate) are rooted in my PhD research. I co-designed *The LEARN Framework* for and with practitioners. Throughout the 7-week professional development training during my PhD study, practitioners used the framework to unpack culturally responsive teaching and design culturally responsive practices. They identified it as the most effective tool when designing culturally meaningful practices.

SECTION 3—Go!
Applying The LEARN Framework for Practice

Section 3 is the culminating section dedicated to unpacking the five principles of *The LEARN Framework*. Each chapter in this section addresses one of the five components of the framework. This section introduces four *practical tools* you can use to design culturally responsive practices. From this section, you will learn what you must know and do to design culturally meaningful practices.

Chapter 5, *The Big Four*, includes four things you need to learn to design culturally responsive practices in sustaining ways. I share *The Big Four* so that you can start designing culturally meaningful practices right away.

Chapter 6, *Start with Why*, discusses the importance of identifying your "why"– *why* you believe you should or should not design and implement culturally meaningful practices. You will learn why identifying your why is perhaps the most important aspect of culturally responsive teaching.

Chapter 7, *The History of Culturally Responsive Education*, discusses the history of culturally responsive education (CRE). Practitioners in my PhD study said they found their *why* after reading about the history of CRE. From this chapter, you will learn that educating students of color and students from low-income communities has a long and contested history. This chapter sheds light on this history; it addresses deficit-based thinking and summarizes why scholars constructed culturally responsive theories.

Chapter 8, *Culturally Meaningful Frameworks*, discusses the work of Gloria Ladson-Billings, Geneva Gay, and Django Paris. From this chapter, you will learn three frameworks you can use as guides to design culturally meaningful practices.

Chapter 9, *Cultural Values and Community Practices*, highlights eight cultural values critical to my work as a practitioner. From this chapter, you will become familiar with cultural values and learn the role culture plays in teaching and learning in the classroom. You will also learn about cultural clashes in the classroom and how clashes lead to academic disengagement among students.

Chapter 10, *Examine*, comprises activities you can engage with to explore your thoughts, feelings, and beliefs about culturally responsive teaching. In this chapter, you will examine your thoughts and feelings about *The Big Four* as you prepare to design culturally responsive practices.

Chapter 11, *Adopt/Apply Culturally Meaningful Frameworks*, prepares you to apply culturally responsive frameworks when designing culturally responsive practices. Throughout this book, I argue that it is impossible to design culturally responsive activities intentionally if you do not use a framework. There are multiple reasons. In this chapter, I provide a useful tool you can use to design culturally responsive practices.

Chapter 12, *Reflect*, includes activities you can engage with to reflect on your designed activity. In this chapter, you will reflect on your designed activity, determine the extent to which the activity engaged students in the classroom, and how you might iterate the lesson to best meet your goals and objectives.

Chapter 13, *Negotiate*, sheds light on negotiating your curriculum with students to design the most effective and responsive practices in the classroom. This chapter discusses the importance of co-planning, co-designing, and co-facilitating activities with students.

SECTION 4—Cooling Down: *Maintaining Your Benefits*

Section 4 concludes with recommendations on what you can do to maintain the many benefits you will gain after reading this book. This section includes only one chapter, Chapter 14.

Chapter 14, *Maintenance*, includes five maintenance activities you can engage with so you do not regress to where you were before reading this book. This chapter includes maintenance tips you can employ to stay on the cutting edge when designing culturally meaningful practices.

Keywords

Community practices

Cultural historical activity theory

Cultural values

Culturally meaningful practices

Culturally relevant pedagogy

Culturally responsive education

Culturally responsive frameworks

Culturally responsive practices

Culturally responsive teaching

Culturally sustaining pedagogy

Deficit-based thinking

Mediation

Theory

Tool use

Introduction:

Culturally Meaningful Practices

———————— ✺ ————————

> ... any [instructional practice] that does not deeply consider culture as the central framework through which learning occurs likely perpetuates inequality.
>
> **—Mahfouz and Anthony-Stevens**

Many books on the market address culture, culturally responsive teaching, and equity. However, few books create opportunities for teachers to achieve agency by engaging in activities and using tools to transform problems that prevent them from designing culturally responsive practices. Instead of creating opportunities for agency, many books, articles, and professional development training on culturally responsive teaching rely on technical quick-tip solutions targeted at students deemed less fortunate, marginalized, and broken.

The central premise of this book is that culturally responsive teaching is achieved through teacher agency, not by implementing quick-tip, technical solutions with Black and Brown students. Teacher agency refers to the role teachers play in their learning. It is the process of *actively engaging* in learning activities— including reading, planning, reflecting, and challenging thoughts and traditional practices, among other activities—to design culturally meaningful and equitable instructional strategies. To achieve agency—to participate in your learning—you need specific tools to assist you along the way.

Most educators fail to achieve agency when considering culturally responsive teaching because their instructional materials are insensitive to students' lived experiences, cultural values, and community practices. Resources insensitive to or ignoring the realities of students contribute to student disengagement and poor teacher-student relationships. Another reason is that professional development trainers often give quick-tip solutions instead of relevant tools teachers could use to participate in their learning. Trainers and popular books rarely provide tools educators could employ to *design* and *redesign* instruction in culturally meaningful ways.

This book defines culturally *meaningful* practices (CMPs) as instructional activities that draw from culturally responsive education (CRE) scholarship. CMPs include culturally *relevant* pedagogy (Ladson-Billings, 1995), culturally *responsive* teaching (Gay, 2014), and culturally *sustaining* pedagogy (Paris, 2012), among other frameworks. I use the term culturally *meaningful* practices to suggest that the practices have *specific meanings* according to particular frameworks. Individuals who lack knowledge of the frameworks and principles may misinterpret the practices in the classroom as chaotic and unproductive.

Teacher Agency in Action

For more than a decade, I have co-planned, co-designed, and co-facilitated culturally meaningful activities with students. These activities placed their cultural values, community practices, and lived experiences at the center of instruction. Students and I have co-designed social and emotional learning (SEL) activities, community building and restorative justice practices, and trauma-informed supports. We have used the arts—including hip-hop, rhythm and blues (R&B), and poetry—to share narratives, process lived experiences, and develop racial and cultural identities.

When planning for groups that integrate hip-hop and the arts with instruction, I intentionally design community-building activities to collect specific information about my students' community practices, lived experiences, and cultural values. Then I use that information to co-design culturally meaningful activities related to their cultural backgrounds. These practices—i.e., hip-hop SEL and trauma-informed supports—have meaning within the context of Paris's (2012) framework (which I introduce in Chapter 8). I employ principles of culturally sustaining pedagogy (Paris, 2012) to design activities for these groups. This is one way of developing culturally meaningful activities through agency. I acted agentically in my learning and professional development by studying Paris's (2012) principles and framework and collaborating with students to co-design culturally sustaining activities.

The Refinement Process

No one taught me how to design culturally responsive practices, and no one provided tools to *guide* me through the design process. Instead, my knowledge came from independent studies on culturally responsive teaching, co-planning activities with students, piloting activities, failing miserably, and iterating practices based on my students' feedback and engagement. Therefore, the following were key to my design process: (1) co-planning with students; (2) trial and error; (3) student feedback; and (4) iterating activities based on student feedback and engagement.

I now call these four components "the refinement process," refining or improving instructional support based on student feedback. We refine by iterating activities to make them more engaging; this contrasts with throwing activities out and discontinuing their use if they fail to produce desired results. When we throw an activity out because it fails to produce desired outcomes, we throw the proverbial baby out in the process. Culturally responsive teaching requires refining our activities based on student feedback, and in this book, I will show you exactly how to do that.

Considering CRE literature is extensive, I had to weed through books and articles to find ideas related to my lesson goals and objectives when designing activities. Like a puzzle, I pieced together principles and theories in culturally meaningful ways. I shared my understanding of principles and theories with my students in simple terms. We created culturally meaningful activities based on our knowledge of various concepts and their predictions on what might be engaging. Notice how my experience with agency starkly contrasts with implementing some quick-tip solution that someone gave me to try out in the classroom. From this perspective, educators achieve agency through agentic actions: actively involving themselves in their learning and professional development and using specific tools to design activities and achieve equity goals.

Tool-use in Achieving Agency

I learned how to design culturally responsive practices over 12 years. Fortunately, now that you have this book, it won't take you anywhere near that long. Depending on where you are on this journey, you may start designing or redesigning instructional activities while reading this book. You may gain insight after reading a few concepts and becoming aware of useful tools; you might use the information and tools within this book right away.

The key to designing culturally meaningful activities is having useful tools you can employ throughout the design process. I often say it is impossible to develop culturally responsive practices *intentionally* if you don't have certain tools. You can't do it. Most trainers on culturally responsive teaching don't train educators on these tools or how to use them. For example, during my PhD research study, all practitioners commented that they never learned specific tools to design culturally meaningful practices; trainers of culturally responsive teaching and graduate training programs never trained them to use tools to develop practices that reflect students' cultures. I included helpful tools and activities within this book so you can design or redesign right away. This book will equip you with four specific tools you will need to create culturally meaningful practices.

Purpose and Benefits of This Book

I wrote this book to provide specific tools you can employ in the classroom to design culturally responsive activities. I cannot overstate the importance of useful resources or tools when creating culturally responsive activities. As I stated earlier, it is impossible to design without knowledge of specific tools. Therefore, this book introduces you to *The LEARN Framework for Practice*, a practical framework that practitioners and I used in my PhD research study to design culturally meaningful activities. This framework:

- clarifies what culturally responsive teaching is and what it is not;
- offers reflection activities related to the history of culturally responsive education, including deficit-based thinking;
- offers four useful tools that practitioners and I co-designed and used to learn about culturally responsive teaching and to design culturally responsive activities;
- compares three prominent culturally meaningful frameworks; and
- guides you through designing culturally meaningful practices—and more.

All educators can design culturally meaningful practices with the right tools and mindset, regardless of race or cultural background. I call *The LEARN Framework* "a framework for practice" because it is designed specifically for practice. Practitioners and I co-designed it to guide stakeholders through applying theories and principles in the classroom to develop culturally meaningful activities. It includes tools to construct culturally meaningful designs in partnership with students. Key features of the framework include:

- culturally meaningful frameworks you can use as guides to design or redesign your practices;
- a community practice survey you can use to identify the cultural values, community practices, and lived experiences of your students;
- a tool to analyze your current practices to determine if your lessons are responsive or insensitive to your students' cultures; and
- a design template to redesign current practices in culturally meaningful ways.

I applaud you for investing time in learning about culturally responsive teaching and designing culturally meaningful instructional practices—and I thank you for considering this book as a resource to access tools for developing culturally meaningful and equitable practices.

The main goal of this book is to give you tools so you can act agentically as you design culturally responsive and equitable practices. Giving you tools contrasts with giving you an array of technical, quick-tip solutions that may not relate to your students' cultural experiences. I am confident that the tools in this book will help you design culturally responsive practices. I aim to create a community of learners dedicated to using *The LEARN Framework* I propose in this book to design culturally meaningful practices. As a community, I hope that we will share our experiences, ask questions, respond to each other's questions, support each other, and work collectively in learning to design quality, culturally meaningful practices for the students we serve.

Community of Learners

To support you along this journey, I have created the *Redesign* private Facebook group so you can connect with and share your learning experiences with other educators using this book to design culturally meaningful activities. To find our community group in Facebook, search *Redesign: An SEL Toolkit for Designing*

Culturally Meaningful Practices. This group gives you the opportunity to process your learning experiences, learn from other educators, access ideas you and your students can adapt, ask questions, get feedback, learn new tools—and more.

Our private community comprises like-minded educators who aspire to design culturally meaningful activities in practical ways. The group's primary goals are for practitioners to support each other on the materials they learn from this book and to access videos and other training materials related to designing culturally meaningful practices.

If you desire a more step-by-step coaching experience, I have designed *The LEARN Academy* to coach you through creating culturally meaningful activities. Within *The Academy*, I walk you through employing the tools I share in this book to design culturally responsive and transformative

- multitiered support systems
- social and emotional learning programming
- trauma informed supports
- special education services
- restorative justice practices—and more!

I felt that providing a private Facebook group for community support would be great for you to join other educators designing culturally meaningful practices. I felt that creating *The Academy* would be great for individuals who desire a more individualized coaching experience. However, this book alone will provide you with essential tools you can use immediately to design culturally responsive practices. The community learning group and *Academy* are additional supports. The activities in this book will provide everything you need to know to re-imagine your practices in culturally meaningful ways. Let's get started by addressing the importance of teacher agency and mediational tools when designing culturally responsive practices, which I do in the next chapter.

SECTION 1

Learners Take Your Mark:
Teacher Agency and Mediational Tools

The concept of agency highlights that actors act by *means* of an environment rather than simply in an environment. To think of agency as achievement makes it possible to understand why an individual can achieve agency in one situation but not in another. To think of agency as achievement rather than as a 'power' also helps to acknowledge that the achievement of agency depends on the availability of economic, cultural, and social resources within a particular ecology. In this sense, we can say that the achievement of agency will always result from the interplay of individual efforts, available resources, and contextual and structural 'factors' as they come together in particular and, in a sense, always unique situations.

—**Biesta and Tedder, 2007**

In this section, you will learn why agency and mediational tools are the heart and soul of culturally meaningful teaching. Without agency and tools, it is impossible to design culturally responsive practices *intentionally* and *purposefully*.

Chapter 1:

Teacher Agency and Mediational Tools

I'm going to use all my tools, my God-given ability, and make the best life I can with it.

—Lebron James

How do you define *teacher agency*? If someone asked you to define *mediational tools*, how would you respond? Take a moment to reflect on your definitions before moving forward. Using the space below, define the terms in your own words. Don't worry if you get stuck; by the end of this chapter, you will be able to define them in your own words. You will know why agency and mediational tools are the heart and soul of designing culturally meaningful practices and why we cannot be effective with culturally meaningful teaching without them.

Teacher Agency Definition:

_____

_____

Mediational Tools Definition:

In the introduction section, I shared my experiences co-designing activities to shed light on how I achieved agency by designing culturally responsive practices over the past 12 years.

In this chapter, I revisit the term *agency* and introduce *mediational tools*, as these two concepts are at the core of my practice as a researcher-practitioner. Agency and mediation are foundational to what I will teach you throughout this book. When I claim that culturally responsive teaching is achieved through agency, I mean it results from actively employing mediational tools to design activities. By the end of this chapter, you will be able to:

- define and explain agency and mediational tools in your own words;
- describe why agency and mediational tools are central to designing culturally meaningful practices;
- articulate why it is *impossible* to design culturally meaningful practices without agency and mediational tools; and
- describe how you will use *The LEARN Framework* throughout this book as a tool to achieve agency with culturally meaningful teaching.

In what follows, I will describe how we will use *The LEARN Framework* as a tool to achieve agency when considering culturally meaningful teaching.

Agency

I started studying agency during my PhD program, and it is a core concept in my PhD research study. Practitioners achieved agency by identifying problems that prevented them from designing culturally responsive practices. Then, they co-designed tools to transform those problems to develop culturally meaningful and justice-oriented SEL activities. Although many things occurred throughout the 7-week PD training, agency was at the core of practitioners' success with designing culturally responsive practices.

There are various ways to define agency, and my goal is not to dictate how you should define it. However, in this book, I describe agency as something we achieve within specific environments by engaging with resources in particular ways to accomplish goals. The direct opposite of agency, according to this definition, is doing absolutely nothing to achieve your goals. It is disengaging from activities and believing you cannot accomplish goals because of specific barriers.

Let's unpack the term by considering business agencies. Business agencies, such as travel agencies, for example, engage in actions and perform tasks to help their clients. Agencies are goal-oriented; instead of waiting for someone to meet the needs of their clients, they engage in specific actions to help their clients achieve goals.

Similarly, agency is taking control of your learning and engaging within environments to transform problems that prevent you from designing culturally meaningful practices. When considering agency, the responsibility is on you; you achieve by using resources within your environment to resolve problems that prevent you from attaining goals. Therefore, agency requires action—it is doing; it is engaging; it is getting your hands dirty; it leads to getting stuck and then unstuck. Ultimately, it leads to learning.

Essentially, through agency, we identify and transform problems that prevent us from designing high-quality instruction for all students. Questions we should consider when discussing agency include:

- What am *I* doing to achieve my goal related to culturally responsive teaching?
- How am *I* helping myself?
- What tools do *I* need to achieve my goal of designing culturally responsive practices?
- Where can *I* find these tools?

Agency is at the core of culturally meaningful teaching and designing culturally meaningful activities. We often receive quick tips and technical solutions from trainers during PD training sessions; it is common to expect coaches to solve our problems by spoon-feeding us information and giving us preplanned, prescriptive, and prepackaged instructional materials to test in the classroom.

However, agency requires that we involve ourselves deeply and take control of our learning to achieve goals and outcomes. How do you think we achieve agency? The answer to this question leads to the second term that guides my work: *mediational tools*. We achieve agency using mediational tools.

Mediational Tools

Mediational tools are resources within our environments that we employ to achieve goals. I'll use a scenario to describe the relationship between agency and meditational tools. For a moment, let's imagine that you move into a new home— your dream home. Imagine that you walk into various rooms in the new house and visualize where you want your furniture. Then, you envision where you want your pictures on the wall. How do you get your furniture to the new home, and how will you get your photos on the wall?

You may rent a U-Haul truck to transport furniture from your previous home to your new home. You may use nails and a hammer or perhaps some adhesive material or tape to achieve the goal of hanging items on the wall. Mediational tools, in these examples, are resources within your environment—things within your community—that you use to help you achieve your goal: the U-Haul, nail, hammer, and adhesive material.

As another example, imagine that, while reading this book, you experience aha moments and want to record your ideas so you don't lose them. What can you use to capture your thoughts? You could use your phone, a notebook, writing utensils, or Word or Google documents. You could also record your thoughts within the margins of this book. These resources are all mediational tools. They play a mediational role in helping you achieve your goal of recording your aha moments and insights.

What mediational tools do you use in your classroom or within your practice? Common tools you might use include:

- pencils
- paper
- computers
- curricula
- videos
- articles
- cultural values
- experience
- language
- internet

Mediational tools help you convey a message or present your instructional lesson; they help you achieve educational goals. Lev Vygotsky, a Russian psychologist who wrote extensively about mediational tools, provided visuals to illustrate how individuals use tools to achieve goals. In Figure 1, I adapt his illustration for this book.

Figure 1: Mediation

Let's unpack this model to understand how we achieve agency through mediational tools. The left point of the triangle represents you; the right point of the triangle represents the goal you wish to achieve. Using this model, how do you achieve the goals you create? You use tools (resources) to help you do something you could not do without the tools. From this perspective, we must find the right tools based on our learning goals and objectives to achieve agency.

Using the LEARN Framework as a Tool to Achieve Goals

I focus on two goals in this book. The first is to unpack culturally responsive teaching, so you will know what it is and is not. The second goal is to provide mediational tools you can use immediately to design culturally meaningful practices. The primary tool to boost your knowledge of culturally responsive teaching is *The LEARN Framework for Practice*. Practitioners and I co-designed the framework during my research study to transform problems that prevented them from designing culturally responsive activities.

Figure 2 is a snapshot of how you will use the framework as a tool to enhance your knowledge of culturally meaningful practices and design culturally meaningful activities.

Figure 2: *The LEARN Framework* as a Mediational Tool

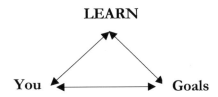

Goals:

1. to understand culturally responsive teaching

2. to design culturally meaningful practices

The LEARN Framework comprises four tools practitioners found useful for unpacking culturally responsive teaching and designing culturally responsive practices within my PhD research study.

These tools included:

1. culturally meaningful frameworks we used to guide our designs;

2. a questionnaire to identify students' interests and community practices;

3. a template to analyze, critique, and problematize current practices (and we used this same tool as a *design template* to re-imagine and re-design current lessons); and

4. a magazine related to the history of culturally responsive education.

We developed tools within the 7-week PD training of my research study. Throughout this book, I will introduce these tools and show you exactly how to use them to design culturally meaningful practices.

The tools practitioners used before the study did not place students' cultural values, lived experiences, or community practices at the center of instruction. We had to design new tools. How do you design culturally meaningful practices if your tools ignore or are insensitive to the lived experiences, cultural values, and community practices of students of color? You can't. That is why, as illustrated in Figure 2, I give you *The LEARN Framework for Practice* as a tool to start designing and redesigning practices in culturally meaningful ways.

Earlier, I stated that this chapter would help you define agency in your own words. Reflect on what you have read about agency. Return to the start of this chapter to review how I define and describe the term. After you reflect on how I define the term, construct a one-sentence definition of agency that you can share if someone asks you to define it. Write your definition in the space below. Don't move on to the next chapter without being able to define agency in your own words.

Agency Definition:

_____

_____

_____

_____

_____

Earlier you defined mediational tools. In the space below, re-define the term, using the insight you've gained from this chapter. Don't move on to the next chapter without being able to define mediational tools in your own words.

Mediational Tools Definition:

_____

_____

_____

During my research study, practitioners remembered terms quicker and were able to incorporate them into their vocabulary when they created their own definitions. They drew from principles and theories and then created definitions of those concepts; in other words, they did not create definitions based on guesswork. Rather, their definitions were rooted in scholarship. Before moving on to the next chapter, be sure that you can define agency and mediational tools in your own words. You will need to know how to explain them when describing your culturally meaningful designs and when coaching your colleagues through the design process.

Summary

In this chapter, I discussed two foundational terms of my work, including (1) agency and (2) mediational tools. These two terms form the basis of this book in that designing culturally meaningful practices requires agency and mediational tools. Agency is involving yourself in your learning within specific environments to achieve desired goals.

Mediational tools are resources within your environment you can access to achieve goals. Drawing from these two terms, I argue that culturally meaningful teaching is achieved through agency; it results from involving yourself in professional development, personal reflection, and employing tools to design culturally meaningful lessons—i.e., culturally *relevant*, culturally *responsive*, or culturally *sustaining* practices, among other culturally meaningful activities— which is precisely what I will show you how to do in this book.

What's Next?

In the next chapter, I share five categories of problems that prevented practitioners from designing culturally meaningful practices throughout the 7-week PD training. I show how, through agency and mediational tools, practitioners transformed problems and designed culturally meaningful SEL activities. The chapter provides an example of how designing culturally meaningful practices results from agency and mediation. By the end of the chapter, you will have greater insight into the importance of using tools to resolve problems and design meaningful practices.

Chapter 2:

In the Beginning was . . . the Problem

Free-Verse Poem

In 2011, I worked as a school psychologist.

Within the first five years of my career, I noticed something that *intrigued* me, something that *confused* me, something that *snatched* my attention.

Teachers read popular books and articles on culturally responsive teaching and attended hours upon hours of training on the topic.

But no matter how many books they read . . .
no matter how many hours of training they received . . .
they *perceived* problems that prevented them from designing culturally responsive activities.

These teachers—my colleagues, my friends—earned bachelor's degrees, master's degrees, and, yeah yall, some y'all even earned doctoral degrees.

But even with these degrees, they lacked confidence in their abilities to form relationships and engage, at a high level, students from diverse ethnicities.

This puzzle, how practitioners experienced problems and struggled, inspired my work with culturally meaningful teaching. It inspired me to earn a PhD degree to explore similar problems.

It inspired me to write this book.

I*n the Beginning was . . . the Problem* is a free-verse poem that my students within my Hip-Hop Social and Emotional Learning (SEL) program inspired me to write. The poem illustrates events and experiences during my tenure as a school psychologist and interventionist. Although practitioners read popular books and received hours of training on culturally responsive teaching, they never learned how to design culturally responsive practices. The books they read and the PD training did not prepare them to design culturally responsive activities specific to their subject areas. This was both intriguing and confusing. It snatched my attention as a young school psychologist. How can educators read books on a subject and receive hours upon hours of training on the topic but struggle to apply the learning in the classroom?

My curiosity motivated me to enroll in the University of Illinois at Chicago's (UIC) PhD curriculum and instruction program to learn more about curriculum studies and examine the problems practitioners experience that prevent them from designing culturally responsive activities. By the 2020–2021 school year, I had finished my PhD classroom coursework and was approved to conduct my PhD research study. I was ecstatic to work closely with teachers and administrators to understand their perceptions of culturally responsive teaching. I was stoked to understand, from their perspective, how it was possible to read popular books and attend hours of training on culturally responsive teaching yet struggle to design culturally responsive practices in the classroom.

In this chapter, I share five categories of problems that prevented practitioners from designing culturally meaningful practices. I describe how they used tools to transform problems to design culturally meaningful activities. By the end of this chapter, you will be able to:

- explain how I define problems that prevent us from designing culturally meaningful activities;
- describe five categories of problems practitioners in my PhD program experienced that prevented them from designing culturally responsive practices;
- recognize the role problems play in preventing us from designing culturally responsive practices; and
- identify why it is necessary to transform problems to design culturally meaningful practices.

From this chapter, you will have greater insight into the role tool mediation plays in culturally responsive teaching, which will prepare you for subsequent chapters on tool use when designing culturally meaningful activities.

Seven-Week PD Training

For my PhD study, I provided a 7-week professional development (PD) training to identify and transform problems that prevented practitioners from designing culturally responsive practices. Seven school-based practitioners participated in the 7-week research study, including school psychologists, social workers, SEL coaches, and administrators. Four of the practitioners were White, and three were Black. The research study focused on "culturally responsive SEL activities" because practitioners had been reading *Culturally Responsive Teaching and the Brain*

(Hammond, 2015), which inspired them to design "culturally responsive SEL community-building activities" to implement in the classroom. They also wanted to coach teachers through designing culturally responsive SEL community-building activities at the Tier 1 level of their multi-tiered support system.

Students were receiving instruction via remote learning because of the COVID-19 pandemic, and educators in the study expressed a desire to learn how to design "culturally responsive SEL activities" to implement in the classroom when students returned to the building. They also wanted to provide "push-in" services, in which they would co-design and implement culturally responsive SEL activities with teachers. Throughout the 7-week training period, practitioners described various problems that prevented them from designing culturally responsive practices. My goal during the 7-week study was to create opportunities for practitioners to identify problems and consider the history of those problems. After identifying and exploring problems, the goal was to co-design and employ meaningful tools they could use to transform problems and design culturally responsive activities.

I was interested in "problems" because, as described in the opening poem of this chapter, although educators read popular books and received hours upon hours of training on the topic, they still struggled to design culturally responsive practices. I was interested in understanding the problems that prevented practitioners from learning to design culturally responsive activities. I defined problems within the study in these ways:

1. challenges/barriers practitioners described with culturally responsive teaching, including lacking knowledge about culturally responsive practices, frameworks, and tenets;

2. challenges/barriers practitioners described in *designing* culturally responsive SEL (CR-SEL) activities, including how to pair SEL and culturally responsive principles to create lessons; and

3. institutional procedures and practices practitioners described as barriers to designing CR-SEL, including school policies and special education law.

I described problems as *any* challenge or barrier that prevented educators from designing culturally responsive practices.

Problem Categories

Throughout the 7-week training, practitioners described 191 problems that prevented them from designing culturally responsive practices. I studied their descriptions of problems, and I placed similar problems into "problem categories." I created a "miscellaneous category," and I used this category to store descriptions of problems that did not fit into problem categories. Following are five problem categories practitioners experienced that prevented them from designing culturally responsive practices at various times during the study:

1. Using Resources that are not Culturally Responsive
2. Experiencing Whiteness
3. Lacking Knowledge Related to Culturally Responsive Teaching
4. Lacking Time to Learn about Culturally Responsive Teaching
5. Experiencing Challenges with Frameworks

Practitioners started the study with various problems that prevented them from designing culturally responsive practices. Throughout the training sessions, we identified and explored these problems, then co-designed and used tools to transform them to develop culturally responsive practices. By the end of the 7-week training, all practitioners analyzed and re-imagined their SEL practices. They did this by co-designing tools to construct SEL activities that placed their students' lived experiences, community practices, and cultural values at the center of instruction. And here is the best part of it all—practitioners learned to design culturally responsive activities by working collectively and acting in their learning.

Practitioners achieved agency using specific tools. Although I conducted the research and facilitated the 7-week PD training, I did not take control of their learning, and I did not give them any technical quick tip solutions to implement with Black and Brown students. Instead, practitioners worked collectively by identifying problems that prevented them from designing culturally responsive practices, and we co-designed tools based on their descriptions of problems. They then used the co-designed tools to transform problems and develop culturally responsive activities.

I describe each category below, and I include excerpts from practitioners so you can understand, in their own words, how they experienced problems that prevented them from designing culturally responsive practices. Their experiences highlight the importance of identifying, exploring, and transforming problems that prevent us from designing culturally meaningful activities. When we transform problems that prevent us from designing culturally meaningful practices, we remove barriers to creating equitable programming.

Category #1: Using Resources that are not Culturally Responsive

Practitioners described using resources not culturally responsive as a problem that prevented them from designing culturally responsive practices. Problems related to this category included using curricula and other instructional materials that did not consider students' cultural values, lived experiences, and community practices. For example, one practitioner commented:

> I was trained in trauma for many, many, many years and including grad school, and then I spent four years at my last school being trained by [professionals] who were very, very well trained in trauma and taught me CBITS [trauma curriculum] and the ins and outs of CBITS . . . and so I felt really strongly about our school becoming a trauma-informed school and

utilizing CBITS because I was trained that it was the best thing to do for kids with trauma, right? And then, over time, just working with Dwayne and researching [culturally responsive teaching], just realizing that parts of CBITS are not culturally responsive. For example, just the communalism pieces, and just having it be so teacher-led, instead of having it be more group-led. And just kind of following a very strict-like instruction and not being as flexible . . . and kind of feeling pressure that I needed to do it this way.

In this excerpt, the participant commented that she could not design culturally responsive practices because she used a trauma-informed curriculum that was strict and inflexible; she commented that parts of the curriculum were not culturally responsive. In response to her comment, another practitioner chimed in:

I have felt since the beginning of SEL that SEL was implemented in the building, in particular, to deal with the behavior problems of Black kids. And so we brought in the Yale RULER approach, which is okay but flawed because it is not culturally relevant, responsive, or anything.

Practitioners commented that the curricula they used were not culturally relevant or responsive to the cultural values or lived experiences of students of color, and this challenge prevented them from designing culturally responsive practices.

Category #2: Experiencing Whiteness

Practitioners described issues related to Whiteness as a problem that prevented them from designing culturally responsive practices. This category included three sub-categories based on how practitioners experienced Whiteness. These categories included:

1. training from a White perspective;
2. being White and implementing culturally responsive practices; and
3. perceiving special education as rooted in Whiteness.

Here is what one practitioner reported related to training from a White perspective:

> I think a large challenge for me is just so much of my training has been from a White perspective for so long. So it's been hard . . . now I'm seeking out what is the best way to support students with trauma from a [culturally responsive teaching] lens or students with anxiety from a [culturally responsive teaching] lens, and I think just finding the right resources . . .

In this example, the participant explained that a significant problem preventing her from designing culturally responsive practices was receiving training from a White perspective. From this view, she commented that her teacher training program ignored the lived experiences, cultural values, and community practices of culturally diverse learners. Her program did not teach her about culturally responsive teaching or culturally meaningful frameworks. Although she read popular books and attended training on culturally responsive teaching, she struggled to find the right tools to assist her in re-designing her practices in culturally meaningful ways.

Here is an example of Being White and Implementing Culturally Responsive Practices:

> . . . But I do think, as I said to Dwayne, no matter how versed we become in [culturally responsive teaching], there is always going to be an additional step, or there's going to be . . . there's going to be things that, from my perspective, as a White person, you're just never going to be able to approach in the same way as a Black staff member. Like, that's just, from my perspective, the way I feel right now.

The practitioner who made this comment shared there were things she would not feel comfortable doing as a White woman. She believed that, because she was White, it would be a challenge to discuss racism with Black students. She also felt uncomfortable discussing racial identity with students of color. She often commented on how, because of her White, middle-class "lens," she would struggle to design effective, culturally responsive practices.

She was not alone, however, in her beliefs about experiencing challenges with culturally responsive teaching because of her Whiteness. Three of the four White practitioners in the study doubted their ability to do certain things related to culturally responsive teaching because of issues associated with Whiteness. Their main concern was addressing race, racism, and challenging injustice with Black students. They felt that Black students would question their motives as White, middle-class women, not take them seriously, and believe their attempt at considering race, culture, and equity in practice was a joke.

Here is an example of Perceiving Special Education as Rooted in Whiteness:

So my mind goes to special education because that's where, you know, I spend most of my time. And I wrote this down because, like . . . where we have to go in the special ed world . . . I just wrote on my form that special education policies and laws are embedded in Whiteness and Eurocentric values . . . and it's like, so extensive, that it's overwhelming because we have to abide by these laws . . . it goes from the assessments, we use [including] rating scales, cognitive assessments . . . in terms of what makes you an intellect. What ADHD means, and the characteristics and the criteria that we then follow . . . that's where I struggle in the special education piece is that we can do whatever we do when we identify at-risk students and put interventions in place, but we're still stuck with this law that's outdated, and how we're identifying students that have disabilities.

In this excerpt, the practitioner described special education as rooted in Whiteness. She commented on having to abide by laws rooted in Eurocentrism and shared that she had to use evaluation tools embedded in Whiteness when evaluating students for special education services. According to the practitioner, this problem prevented her from designing culturally responsive practices. Her main argument was that even with culturally responsive practices, she would have to use culturally insensitive tools to evaluate students if teachers referred them for special education services. She commented that this problem was embedded in special education law and that there was nothing she could do about it.

Category #3: Lacking Knowledge Related to Culturally Responsive Teaching

Practitioners described lacking knowledge related to culturally responsive teaching as a problem that prevented them from designing culturally responsive practices. The following excerpt is an example of lacking knowledge of culturally responsive teaching.

> I feel like I don't have a strong, like . . . if someone asked me what the definition [of culturally responsive teaching] was, like, I don't think I would have a good straightforward definition. . . . And I've never designed any CR [culturally responsive] activities or seen anyone else do it. I just need help, Dwayne!

In this excerpt, the participant commented that a significant problem that prevented her from designing culturally responsive practices was that she did not have a solid definition of culturally responsive teaching. Other problems were that she had seen no one develop culturally responsive practices or implement culturally responsive activities in the classroom.

Lacking knowledge related to culturally responsive teaching prevented practitioners from designing culturally responsive practices. And guess what—

receiving technical tips and tricks from previous training sessions did not transform their underlying problems. The real challenge that prevented them from designing culturally responsive practices was that they had never seen culturally responsive teaching in action, and they had no design models they could use to guide them through the design process. Although they received quick-tip solutions, they had no idea how those solutions were culturally meaningful to their students, and they lacked knowledge of what made those quick-tip solutions culturally meaningful according to culturally responsive education (CRE) scholarship.

Category #4: Lacking Time to Learn About Culturally Responsive Teaching

Practitioners described lacking time as a problem that prevented them from designing culturally responsive practices. The following excerpt is an example of lacking time.

> I think, as with most everything in education, the biggest barrier is time: time to learn, time to reflect, time to create, time to analyze, time to adjust, and time to improve. Designing culturally responsive activities is a huge investment of time that I know is worth the price, but there are still only 24 hours in the day.

Practitioners commented on the challenges they experienced with time. Because they had no time during the day to unpack culturally responsive teaching and design culturally responsive activities, they stated that they could not redesign their practices in culturally meaningful ways. Their time was consumed by their day-to-day work with students and working in problem-solving teams to address challenges concerning academics, behavior, and attendance.

Category #5: Experiencing Challenges with Frameworks

Practitioners described experiencing challenges with frameworks as a problem that prevented them from designing culturally responsive practices. The following excerpt is an example of this kind of problem.

> . . . So I originally went with the culturally relevant pedagogy [framework] and kind of did all of you know, filled out how I am helping them achieve this. And then I really got stuck with number three [tenet]. And Dwayne and I talked a little bit and it's really like because it's such a structured curriculum . . . I wasn't sure how to do this. And then, it made me think that maybe I picked the wrong framework.

As practitioners learned about culturally responsive frameworks, they described problems related to specific tenets of the framework. Throughout the 7-week training, however, practitioners identified problems, and as a collective, we co-designed tools to address those problems. By the end of the training sessions, all practitioners designed culturally responsive practices, using four specific tools throughout the study. The following excerpt is a comment a practitioner shared about learning to design culturally responsive practices:

> I do feel that I can run culturally responsive sessions now and that I have enough of an understanding and methods to implement the work, but I wish I was doing this work sooner . . . The [7] week [research study] sessions are the most growth I have had as a practitioner since I began working at my current school.

By the end of the 7-week study, one of the participants commented that she experienced additional problems as she learned about culturally responsive practices. However, she relied on a tool we used in the study to guide her through the design process. In her words:

Lack of knowledge was my initial concern along with not having a lot of time to focus on [culturally responsive teaching]. As the study continued, my concerns evolved to "How do I apply this to each situation?" I then decided to just focus on the table [a tool] and use that to guide me through each situation.

The five categories in this chapter represent underlying problems that prevented practitioners from designing culturally responsive practices. Notice that quick-tip, technical solutions do not address these problems; practitioners stated that previous books and training sessions did not focus on the problems that prevented them from designing culturally responsive practices. Throughout the 7-week study, practitioners achieved agency by employing tools to transform their problems. They read articles related to the problems they experienced; co-designed a survey to identify their students' community practices; analyzed, critiqued, and problematized their lesson plans; and used culturally responsive frameworks to guide re-design practices. Practitioners re-imaged their practices as they transformed problems that prevented them from designing culturally responsive activities. Agency and tool mediation were central to re-imagining their practices.

Summary

During my early years as a school psychologist, I was intrigued and puzzled by the fact that practitioners read popular books and articles on culturally responsive teaching. Educators received hours upon hours of training on the topic but struggled to design culturally responsive practices. This inspired me to study the problems that prevent practitioners from creating culturally responsive practices. To explore the difficulties that practitioners experienced, I provided PD training for seven educators to identify and examine the problems that prevented them from designing culturally responsive practices.

Practitioners described a host of problems that I placed into five "problem" categories, including: (1) using resources that are not culturally responsive; (2) experiencing Whiteness; (3) lacking knowledge related to culturally responsive teaching; (4) lacking time to learn about culturally responsive teaching; and (5) experiencing challenges with frameworks. Practitioners acted in agentic ways in their learning as they used mediational tools to transform problems and designed culturally meaningful SEL activities.

What's Next?

In the next chapter, I address a problem that many educators experience concerning culturally responsive teaching. I attack this problem so you don't experience similar challenges while reading this book. Culturally responsive teaching has various names that sound similar and can be confusing. For example, practitioners in my research study said that it was challenging to determine which framework to use based on various objectives. They were unsure if they should consider culturally relevant pedagogy (Ladson-Billings, 1995), culturally responsive teaching (Gay, 2014), culturally sustaining pedagogy (Paris, 2012), or other culturally meaningful frameworks. In the next chapter, I address these problems so that culturally responsive teaching names do not confuse you!

SECTION 2

Get Ready: *Understanding Theoretical Frameworks*

We use theory to understand what is happening around us and to describe what and why things are happening the way they are . . . sometimes, we use theory to prescribe how to achieve certain effects.

—Susan McKenny

In this section, you will learn about the benefits of using theoretical frameworks to design culturally meaningful practices. You'll learn why it is impossible to design culturally responsive activities *intentionally* and *purposefully* without theories and frameworks.

Chapter 3:

The Meaning is in The Framework

I don't know if this is an actual issue, but trying to figure out a way to assess whether I would need to utilize culturally responsive teaching, culturally [relevant] pedagogy, or culturally sustaining pedagogy, and which one is best for a given situation . . . That's why I just keep tripping up quite a bit on like, how do you assess which one [framework] is most important for the situation.

—PhD Research Participant

We have all heard of culturally responsive teaching. Depending on how long you have studied culturally responsive education (CRE) scholarship, you may be familiar with culturally relevant pedagogy (Ladson-Billings, 1995). If you are like practitioners in my study—and thousands of other educators I have trained—you have no idea what culturally *sustaining* pedagogy is or which framework to use when designing "culturally responsive practices."

In this chapter, I discuss the importance of names within culturally responsive teaching scholarship, particularly the names of theoretical frameworks. I do this because I have trained teachers new to the field of culturally responsive teaching as well as teachers seasoned in the practice. No matter where they were on their journey, they experienced problems with the "names" of theories, principles, and frameworks.

When they learned about frameworks, they became confused about which one to use based on specific learning goals and outcomes. To design culturally meaningful practices with confidence, they needed to understand frameworks and know which framework to use based on their goals and objectives. By the end of this chapter, you will be able to:

- articulate the importance of framework names and what they suggest;
- describe why a framework's name has implications for practice; and
- articulate how using the phrase "culturally meaningful practices" resolved confusion practitioners experienced in my study, and why it will help you too.

Lamont (pseudonym), a seasoned African American male social worker who participated in my study, acknowledged that teasing out the many names of frameworks within the CRE scholarship can be confusing. He argued that it's challenging to know when to use a particular framework in practice based on specific goals and objectives. I included his response in the opening quote of this chapter to illustrate this problem. One way of dealing with the problem that Lamont and others in my study described was to design activities that allowed practitioners to understand how frameworks are similar to and different from each other—and how frameworks are meaningful in their own right. To know how culturally meaningful frameworks are similar to and different from each other, I needed to teach them what is "in the name" of culturally meaningful frameworks, which is what you will learn in this chapter.

What is in the Name?

Consider the following story to understand the importance of names when learning about culturally meaningful teaching and designing culturally meaningful practices. Hollie (2019) received an article to review for an online publication. The article's title was *Culturally relevant leadership: What does it take?* (p. 32). As Hollie read and reread the article, he searched for key aspects and assumptions of "culturally relevant leadership" based on the title of the article.

The article's title, the name "Culturally relevant leadership," was misleading. Instead of identifying key assumptions, constructs, and principles related to culturally relevant leadership in the article, Hollie (2019) commented that the author sprinkled an array of buzzwords like "equity," "cultural sensitivity," and "inclusivity" (p. 32). Hollie (2019) explained that, while the author used the name "culturally relevant" in the title, the article did not address culturally relevant literature, culturally relevant principles, or culturally relevant frameworks.

In response to this experience, Hollie (2019) asked a thought-provoking question that practitioners and I unpacked for an entire training session. His question was, "What is in a name?" (p. 32). What is in the name culturally *relevant* pedagogy? What is in the name culturally *responsive* teaching? What is in the name culturally *sustaining* pedagogy? What is in the name of other culturally meaningful frameworks?

What is the meaning of these names—culturally *relevant*, culturally *responsive*, culturally *sustaining*—and why did scholars use them to describe their framework? Hollie (2019) argues that a name or theory is associated with a specific theoretical framework that details the relevance of the theory. To Hollie's (2019) point, when designing culturally responsive practices, it is necessary to understand what is in the name to understand the practice. I'll share another story to illustrate this point, a story like Hollie's (2019) experience.

The year was 2010. I had graduated from Marshall University Graduate College, where I spent four years studying the impact of culture on academic engagement.

My passion for scholarship that addressed race, culture, and equity inspired me to conduct a study titled *Effects of Cultural Characteristics in School on Academic Engagement.* I designed tools to measure cultural values within classrooms (I discuss these values in Chapter 9), and I used those tools to observe 18 classrooms in two high school buildings in the Midwest U.S.A. Three hundred twenty students participated in the study.

This was my first year as a school psychologist and my first time co-designing culturally responsive practices with students; my thesis study significantly affected my practices. Instead of implementing prepacked, prescriptive, and preplanned curricula, I co-designed practices with students, based on their lived experiences, cultural values, and community practices.

Practitioners observed how students responded to intervention support groups that incorporated students' cultures and experiences and requested training on my thesis research topic and work with culturally meaningful teaching. Principals in my district requested that I train their teachers on culturally "relevant" teaching. They wanted me to train teachers on "culturally relevant response-to-intervention," (RTI) to be exact. During this time (2010–2011 school year), practitioners were learning how to design RTI service delivery models, and they wanted to learn how to make their RTI practices culturally *relevant.*

When I trained teachers on these topics, they used the phrase culturally relevant teaching as educators use culturally "responsive" teaching today. When I trained them, they did not know why scholars used terms such as culturally *relevant* or culturally *responsive.* They knew that the practice had something to do with making instruction "relevant" and/or "responsive" to the cultures of "students of color." All practitioners had heard of culturally *relevant* teaching, and some had heard of culturally *responsive* practices.

One day, while training practitioners on culturally relevant RTI processes, one teacher described practices using Gay's (2014) principles and framework. However, instead of saying she implemented "culturally responsive practices" as defined in

Gay's (2014) framework, she kept calling the practices "culturally relevant," and she cited "Ladson-Billings" as the source she used to design the activities. One of the other teachers familiar with Ladson-Billings' (1995) and Gay's (2014) work pointed out this confusion. She asked for clarity. She wanted to know whether the practices were designed using Ladson-Billings' (1995) principles or Gay's (2014) principles. This question was brilliant because it suggested that names, principles, and assumptions give meaning to frameworks.

A framework's name describes the practice the framework aims to produce. For example, practices designed after Ladson-Billings' (1995) framework would look a particular way and include specific learning objectives (that stakeholders create) based on the principles of her framework. Learning goals and objectives would be meaningful based on her framework. The same is true for all other culturally meaningful frameworks. The point is—the *meaning* is in the framework. If you lack knowledge of the framework, you won't understand how classroom activities are culturally *relevant, responsive,* or *sustaining* because the framework's name points to the practice the framework aims to design.

It is essential to acknowledge that the names of frameworks have a specific meaning based on principles that comprise the framework. Practitioners found the phrase "culturally responsive practices" (CRP) confusing after learning there are an array of frameworks and principles. For example, after studying Ladson-Billings' (1995), Gay's (2014), and Paris's (2012) frameworks, they felt that the wording "culturally responsive" made them think about Gay's principles, considering the name of her work (culturally *responsive* teaching). Historically, scholars have used the term *culturally responsive practices* to describe a body of teaching practices that intentionally integrate the cultural references, assets, literacies, heritages, and lived experiences of students with instruction (Gay, 2018; Ladson-Billings, 1995).

However, based on the challenges teachers in my study experienced, I taught the frameworks separately, based on the definitions and principles that comprise each of the three frameworks (culturally *relevant* pedagogy, Ladson-Billings, 1995;

culturally *responsive* teaching, Gay, 2014; and culturally *sustaining* pedagogy, Paris, 2012). I then brought the frameworks together to show that, although they all have common goals, each framework has a specific meaning based on particular principles that comprise the framework. To help practitioners understand this concept, I recommended that they design culturally *meaningful* activities. Creating culturally meaningful practices or activities meant that practitioners would pull from either Ladson-Billings' (1995), Gay's (2014), and/or Paris's (2012) framework to design practices and then show what makes the practice *culturally meaningful* based on the framework they used and their students' experiences.

The key in their designs was in the meaning—how practitioners made sense of their designs concerning principles that guided them. How practitioners described their designs—based on their understanding of culturally meaningful frameworks—provided insight into my research question and helped me understand and reflect on their learning related to frameworks. From this approach, I recommended that they design culturally meaningful activities instead of describing all practices as "culturally responsive" as a general phrase to illustrate culturally relevant, responsive, *and* sustaining activities. I shared that the meaning of their activities will be in the framework they select to guide them through the design process.

This meant that practitioners would have to explain the framework and the principles that give it meaning, and then they would have to share how their designs were meaningful to their students' cultures and experiences. This activity was effective at helping practitioners understand that culturally responsive education is replete with definitions, principles, and frameworks that point to culturally meaningful teaching. It also helped them understand that frameworks are "remixed"—that scholars who construct culturally meaningful theories borrow from previous theories in the field, which is why many frameworks have common goals and similar principles. They also learned, however, that frameworks were unique in that the principles that comprise them make them special. They discovered that guiding principles, which you will learn in Chapter 8, give meaning to frameworks.

Ultimately, by the end of the training, instead of calling all practices that address culturally meaningful activities "culturally responsive practices," practitioners described culturally *meaningful* practices based on specific principles and frameworks. They learned that all frameworks have specific meanings because the meaning is in the framework. When you learn about frameworks in Chapter 8, you'll realize that your framework knowledge will guide you through designing activities related to principles that comprise the framework. You will learn explaining your practices to others is simply describing principles of the framework you used and how you used those principles to design activities based on your students' experiences.

Therefore, while it is common to use the phrase "culturally responsive practices" to describe an array of instructional approaches associated with culturally responsive education (CRE), I use the term culturally *meaningful* practices to describe instructional activities that draw from one or more frameworks—i.e., culturally *relevant*, culturally *responsive*, culturally *sustaining*, and so on. I use the phrase culturally meaningful to acknowledge that these practices have meaning based on a specific framework. The framework could be any culturally meaningful framework within the CRE literature. From this perspective, the meaning of the designed activity is centered on the framework and students' experiences. Therefore, in subsequent chapters, when you read the phrase "culturally meaningful practices," "culturally meaningful activities," or "culturally meaningful teaching," know that the term refers to specific practices that have meaning in a particular framework.

To avoid confusion, I will identify the framework's name when I comment on a particular framework. For example, suppose my goal is to describe practices related to culturally *relevant* pedagogy (Ladson-Billings, 1995). Here, I will not call these activities culturally "responsive" practices, although scholars in the field use such terminology. Instead, I will call them culturally "relevant" practices, consistent with Ladson-Billings (1995) principles and framework, which gives this framework, and thus activities, meaning. When I describe practices related to culturally *responsive* teaching (Gay, 2014), I am speaking specifically about four principles I include in this book (see Chapter 8), principles related to Gay's (2014) culturally responsive teaching framework.

If my goal is to describe practices related to culturally *sustaining* pedagogy (Paris, 2012), I will not call these culturally "relevant" or "responsive" practices; I will call them culturally "sustaining" practices, which suggests that the designed activities are associated with principles from culturally sustaining pedagogy (Paris, 2012). I use the phrase culturally meaningful teaching and culturally meaningful practices/activities to suggest that the teaching/practices mean specific things within the context of particular frameworks. If you are unfamiliar with the frameworks, then you will not know how the activity or practice is culturally meaningful according to those frameworks. Consequently, the activities would appear chaotic and unproductive to you in the classroom because you lack knowledge and awareness of culturally meaningful teaching, principles, and frameworks.

If you understand the framework, however, you can point out the principles of the framework in practice, and you can observe culturally meaningful activities—aligned with the framework—in action. Therefore, in this book, I use the phrases "culturally meaningful teaching" and "culturally meaningful practices/activities" to represent teaching practices that draw from frameworks within the field of CRE. Figure 3 illustrates the relationship between culturally meaningful frameworks and practices.

Figure 3: Culturally Meaningful Frameworks and Culturally Meaningful Practices

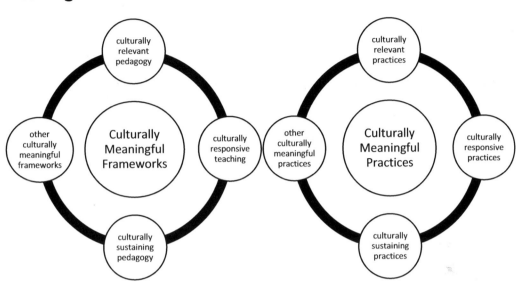

Practitioners from my study taught me it is vital to address the issue of "names"—names of culturally meaningful frameworks—when learning about culturally meaningful teaching and designing culturally meaningful practices. Although I coach practitioners on the differences and similarities of each of the three frameworks mentioned above, it is essential to know that, when considering CRE, it is best practice to consider the frameworks as building upon each other rather than as isolated, fragmented frameworks and practices. Gloria Ladson-Billings (2014) calls building on other frameworks "remixing," in which scholars use theories and principles from other established frameworks and then "remix" those frameworks to make new ones to meet the changing needs of students (p. 76).

Culturally responsive framework names are less likely to confuse you now that you are aware that culturally responsive teaching comprises a host of theories, principles, and frameworks, and now that you know each framework has a specific meaning based on principles that form the framework.

Summary

In this chapter, I shed light on a common problem related to culturally responsive teaching. This problem is related to names. When learning about frameworks in my PhD research study, practitioners were confused by the many terms that scholars use to describe culturally responsive teaching, including culturally *relevant* pedagogy, culturally *responsive* teaching, and culturally *sustaining* pedagogy. I explained the importance of knowing what the names of frameworks mean. I use the phrase culturally *meaningful* teaching and culturally *meaningful* practices/activities to convey that practices are rooted in frameworks composed of specific principles. In other words, names and principles matter when designing culturally meaningful practices.

What's Next?

In the next chapter, I describe the historical development of *The LEARN Framework* that practitioners and I co-designed and used to construct culturally meaningful practices. Knowing *The LEARN Framework* helps you understand how the framework is rooted in history, research, and practice. You will learn how to describe it when sharing it as a tool to design culturally meaningful practices. Practitioners in my study commented that they lacked knowledge of frameworks. Their experiences inspired me to include *The Historical Development of The LEARN Framework* as a chapter so that when you use the framework, you will know about its history, and you'll be able to explain to others how it is rooted in history, research, and practice.

Chapter 4:

The Historical Development of The LEARN Framework

———— ·∞· ————

> Theory without practice is of little value, whereas practice is the proof of theory. Theory is the knowledge; practice is the ability.
>
> **—Alois Podhajsky**

What comes to mind when you hear the term *theoretical framework*? How do you define the term? Share your thoughts below.

Theoretical Framework Definition:

_____

_____

_____

As a school-based practitioner, I am keenly aware of how much we, as educators, despise theory and theoretical frameworks. For example, I have worked with educators who said they did not want to be a part of equity teams because they did not want to "waste their time discussing theory." I understand the frustration that school-based practitioners experience concerning theory. We are school-based practitioners, not theoreticians, right? Wrong!

As practitioners, we theorize about our practices when describing our work with colleagues, sharing specific steps to achieve a task, and describing problems on the board with students in the classroom and during meetings with parents and colleagues. We use theory to guide our practices when we design lessons, and we use frameworks as guides when planning activities. We construct frameworks— although we do not call them "frameworks"—when helping students and teachers achieve tasks. Since we use frameworks indirectly in our practices as practitioners, why do many of us frown upon theory and frameworks? Based on my experiences, the answer is many practitioners have not been taught the proper definition of theories and frameworks. There is a relationship between theory and practice because theories shape practices, and practices shape theory.

In this chapter, I discuss the historical development of *The LEARN Framework for Practice*, the framework that practitioners and I co-designed and used in my PhD research study to guide them as they designed culturally meaningful activities. By the end of this chapter, you will be able to:

- describe how practitioners and I co-designed *The LEARN Framework*;
- identify how the framework is rooted in research;
- recognize why the framework is a "framework for practice"; and
- articulate why the framework creates opportunity for student agency, negotiation in the classroom, and collaboration among students and teachers.

I shed light on the historical development of the framework, so you will know how practitioners and I coined the framework and understand how the framework is rooted in history, research, and practice. I dispel myths related to theory and practice so you will understand why theories and theoretical frameworks are essential tools you will use to design culturally meaningful practices.

The Historical Development of the *LEARN Framework*

Before conducting my PhD study, I spent months reading articles and reflecting on ideas I could use within the study to guide practitioners through designing culturally responsive practices. After reviewing the literature and reflecting on culturally responsive teaching concepts, I reflected on my practices and experiences with culturally responsive teaching. I paired the literature review with my practices. My main goal in this process was to develop professional development training content to share with educators for the intervention study I planned to conduct for my dissertation.

Before conducting the study, I had trained educators on culturally responsive teaching for over a decade. From the training sessions, I found that educators responded positively to specific parts of the training. For example, when I shared certain information during PD sessions, practitioners often engaged with the content at a high level and shared their narratives related to the information. I documented these components and studied them.

I wanted to spend more time during training sessions on concepts educators found useful for unpacking culturally responsive teaching. I tried to remove all the "fluff" from my training sessions and spend more time on ideas that practitioners found challenging to understand. Essentially, developing *The LEARN Framework* was combing through concepts, activities, and narratives I shared with teachers and identifying components of my training that were most effective at creating aha moments. This was studying my training materials to identify elements that practitioners found insightful—components of my training that gave practitioners a renewed interest in culturally responsive teaching.

Here is how I did it. After training educators on my approach to culturally responsive teaching, I asked for feedback. I provided evaluation forms for educators to complete after my training sessions to document whether my training met their needs and whether the content and activities met the objectives and purpose of the training session. I also asked for feedback on parts of the training that were most insightful and the most confusing aspects of the training.

From this process, educators from different schools, districts, and states identified similar content that made things click for them. They also identified similar presentation aspects that renewed their interest in culturally responsive teaching. After studying these components and documenting how educators responded to them, I interviewed teachers and administrators about my training to see if they would provide similar or different responses than the educators I had surveyed. When I met with them, I began with an open-ended discussion about the training: "Please tell me your thoughts about the training." I then got more specific. I asked an array of questions like:

- What were the most effective components of the training for you?
- What parts of the training were most confusing for you?
- What questions do you still have about culturally responsive teaching and designing culturally responsive activities I did not address during the session?

From this process, I had a range of responses and questions that educators were still confused about, questions that educators needed to answer to better understand culturally responsive teaching and to prepare to design culturally responsive activities. During the 2020–2021 school year, I provided training via Zoom to hundreds of educators, including administrators. This opportunity was timely because it gave me feedback from hundreds of teachers across subject areas; I also got feedback from administrators on aspects of my training.

I spent months studying how educators responded to my training content. After training educators via Zoom, I printed the chat responses, which provided pages of transcripts to study. I read through the transcripts and highlighted parts of the PD that educators seemed to find most helpful. I also highlighted aspects of the transcripts that participants seemed to need more time learning. I then compared these responses to the interviews I gathered and educators' evaluation feedback from previous training sessions.

During the 2019–2020 school year, a few of my colleagues offered to assist with a Zoom training I facilitated. As I provided Zoom PD training, they managed the breakout rooms, monitored the chat responses, and highlighted questions that participants typed in the chat space during the training. My colleagues were familiar with my training materials; before assisting me with the breakout rooms and chat responses, they had attended 8 hours of my training sessions and were aware of my presentation's structure.

Considering my colleagues facilitated breakout sessions during the Zoom events, I met with them after the training sessions to get their thoughts on how participants responded to the training content. I asked them these questions:

- What parts of the PD seemed most effective at helping educators understand culturally responsive teaching?
- What parts of the training do you think educators responded most favorably to—which parts led to "aha moments?"
- What parts should I remove because of time constraints?
- What questions did educators share during breakout sessions?
- What questions did educators share during breakout sessions that we did not have time to answer?

After this process, I shared with educators who facilitated the breakout rooms a visual that I had created. The graphic illustrated my training activities. It included components educators believed were most effective at simplifying culturally responsive education. It also had components based on the most frequently asked questions from educators, based on interviews and evaluation feedback.

When I shared this information with my colleagues, I included seven components or "themes" that comprised best practices when training on culturally responsive education based on teacher feedback. I asked my colleagues who assisted me with training if they would organize my training materials and create an acronym from my seven components. I gave them the seven components that comprised my training, and I included training activities I typically include within each of the seven components. One of the participants in the study, Sasha (pseudonym), an administrator and SEL coach, took all seven elements and sorted the content and activities into four categories to create the acronym *LEAR*. *LEAR* stood for *L*earn, *E*xamine, *A*dopt/*A*pply, and *R*eflect (I will discuss these components in Chapters 6-12).

Sasha was much better than I at organizing ideas into bite-sized topics and acronyms, and she was brilliant at synthesizing information in memorable ways. Her concept of *LEAR* comprised all seven elements of my work. Still, I felt there was a missing component, and I believed this component was one reason educators struggled to design culturally responsive practices. I thought this missing element was why students disengaged at alarming rates during instructional time.

As I reflected on the missing piece, I thought about how students often described their learning experiences. They repeatedly stormed into my office, dragged chairs and placed them next to my desk, and said things like, "Oh my goodness, Dr. Williams, class be super boring! I be sittin' there goin' to sleep, starin' at my phone, starin' at the clock. I swear I be waitin' for the bell to ring! Oh my goodness—I hate that class!"

As I thought about these experiences, I thought about my work with culturally responsive community-building activities and SEL counseling groups. I thought about how creating opportunities for students to co-plan, co-design, and co-lead activities and opportunities for them to share their voices in the classroom were the most effective aspects of my work as a practitioner. As I reflected on my students' stories related to their experiences in the classroom and thought about how practical co-designing activities with students were, I felt this component should be a part of the framework. I thought the framework was incomplete because it did not include student participation and students' voice.

The missing component of the framework was that it did not address the need to create opportunities for student agency. For example, it did not create opportunities for students to co-plan, co-design, and co-facilitate activities in the classroom. Therefore, I added the letter *N* to *LEAR* to make the acronym *LEARN*. The letter *N* refers to *negotiate* and implies a multi-voiced process of designing instructional activities by which students and teachers collectively negotiate by co-planning, co-designing, and co-leading activities in the classroom.

By co-planning, co-designing, and co-leading activities, students would have an opportunity to insert their cultural values, lived experiences, and community practices into the lesson and learning environment. The letter *N* component of the framework, from my experiences working with students, was the most effective component at boosting engagement among students in general and culturally diverse learners in particular because activities were products of their interests, values, and designs. I was convinced, based on my experiences co-designing activities with students across tiers, that the letter *N* was the most practical compared to all other *LEARN* framework elements.

Although practitioners and I organized *The LEARN Framework* and planned to use the five components during my PhD research study, we could only use the first three elements—LEA—because my research study did not include working directly with students. My study included working with adults only. During the study, we could not employ the letters *R* and *N*—*reflecting* on designed practices and *negotiating* with students—of the framework. Therefore, content related to the letters *LEA* within this book draws from experiences coaching practitioners on culturally meaningful practices before this study and practitioners' experiences during the study. Letters *R* and *N* within this book draw from my practices as an equity coach and school psychologist, designing culturally meaningful practices since 2011.

I won't discuss each component of *The LEARN Framework* in this chapter. Instead, I unpack each component in subsequent chapters; I dedicate a chapter to each letter to explain what the letter represents and introduce activities you can use to engage with the letter. It is essential to know that the five action-oriented components of the framework (*LEARN*) are not linear; practitioners do not have to follow the components in order. Rather, they may move through the elements while learning about culturally meaningful teaching and designing. For example, although the letter *N* in the framework is the last letter in the acronym, practitioners and students can negotiate activity elements throughout the process with each framework element. Practitioners can also start the design process by negotiating their classes' syllabi and curriculum activities.

I shared ideas with my colleagues regarding the letter *N* (negotiate), and we discussed its relevance to the *LEARN* acronym and process. We agreed that the framework was sufficient to design activities based on its five principles. We felt confident considering our experience with the framework concepts and the evaluation and interview feedback from school-based practitioners. Using the first three components of the framework—*LEA*—I designed a prototype online course with feedback from educators who helped organize *The LEARN Framework*. Then, I introduced the course to practitioners who participated in the study.

We then used the framework to learn about culturally responsive teaching and design culturally meaningful practices. The greatest benefit of the framework is that it guides practitioners through understanding culturally responsive education from a historical perspective, and it steps practitioners through designing culturally meaningful activities. Now that you know about its historical development, we will unpack each framework component in subsequent chapters. Then, I will walk you through using the framework to understand culturally meaningful teaching and design engaging, culturally meaningful activities.

Summary

I co-designed *The LEARN Framework for Practice* with four educators who participated in my PhD research study. One educator organized my training materials into a 4-step process, and she used the acronym *LEAR* to describe the activities within each component—*L*earn, *E*xamine, *A*dopt/*A*pply, and *R*eflect. I felt students' voices were missing from the *LEAR* framework, and I included the letter *N*(negotiate) to address this concern. Then, I organized activities within *The LEARN Framework* with my colleagues' feedback. I used the framework during my PhD research study to help educators understand culturally responsive teaching and design culturally responsive practices. Using the framework as a guide, practitioners designed culturally meaningful SEL activities, placing the lived experiences, community practices, and cultural values at the center of SEL programming.

What's Next?

In the next chapter, I introduce the letter *L* of *The LEARN Framework*, which stands for learn. Specifically, I discuss *The Big Four*, four things educators in my study needed to learn to design culturally responsive practices. Letter *L* was the first component practitioners and I unpacked during the study. It is an essential component of the framework because, historically, institutions—including teacher education programs—have excluded the lived experiences, cultural values, and community practices of culturally diverse learners from their syllabi. Educators now lack information regarding culturally diverse learners, and thus, struggle to design culturally meaningful activities.

The letter *L* of the framework, *The Big Four*, will bring you up to speed with what culturally responsive teaching is and what it is not. I will share why this is the most important starting place when unboxing culturally responsive teaching and learning to design culturally responsive activities. I draw from my work with students on the ground level, my experiences as an equity coach, and my experiences as a researcher, studying problems that prevent practitioners from designing culturally meaningful practices.

SECTION 3

Go! *Applying The LEARN Framework*

The new "additional" problem that emerged for me after learning more about [culturally responsive teaching] was that I tend to box myself into one version of [culturally responsive teaching] - Geneva Gay's culturally responsive teaching because that is what I find to be the easiest to recall by memory as well as because to me that seems to be the most realistic to implement across various content areas. However, the more that I develop within the world of [culturally responsive teaching], I need to be careful not to pigeonhole myself into that framework, as both Gloria Ladson-Billings and Django Paris's frameworks have merit. In particular, as I progress with my own skills in [culturally responsive teaching], I need to push myself to move out of my comfort zone more into Paris's culturally sustaining framework rather than sitting comfortably in the middle of the three. As a White woman, I need to push forward in my [culturally responsive teaching] development even amidst my own self-doubt because my students deserve to have an education that not only values their identities but helps them to make this world better by critiquing the status quo.

—PhD Research Participant

In this section, I unpack each element of *The LEARN Framework for Practice*, the framework practitioners and I co-designed and used to learn about and design culturally meaningful activities during my 7-week PhD research study. Each letter of the framework is an action-step you must take to become competent at designing culturally meaningful practices.

Get ready to take notes. Get ready to debunk practices that interfere with culturally responsive teaching. Get ready to re-imagine your work in culturally meaningful ways!

Chapter 5:

The Big Four

———————— ∞ ————————

I think the time we first spent understanding the background of [culturally responsive teaching], including the history and purpose of [it] as well as many of the prominent frameworks was crucial to my development in becoming a culturally responsive practitioner.

—PhD Research Participant

Now that you know *The LEARN Framework's* historical development and understand this book is rooted in research and practice, I will unpack *The LEARN Framework* we used in my study to design culturally responsive practices. While writing this book, it was challenging to determine what to include and exclude in each chapter because I had rich experiences during my study. I wanted to share them all with you in this book.

Initially, I wanted to show you the entire process of *identifying, exploring,* and *transforming* problems to design culturally responsive practices, the same process that practitioners and I took in my study to transform problems and develop culturally responsive activities. However, I decided against this, as the goal of this book is to keep it short and simple. Most importantly, I want to give you practical tools you can use immediately to design and redesign your practices in culturally meaningful ways.

As I reflected on how to best prepare you for culturally meaningful teaching, I focused on a common problem that practitioners in my study described. I also focused on problems that prevent thousands of educators from designing culturally responsive practices. That problem is lacking knowledge of culturally responsive teaching. No matter where I go in the country when I train educators on culturally responsive teaching, teachers say something like, Dwayne—

- I want to design culturally responsive practices, but I am unsure what culturally responsive teaching is.
- I want to design culturally responsive practices, but I have no idea where to start.
- I want to design culturally responsive practices, but I have never seen it done.

These responses fall within the category of lacking knowledge of culturally responsive teaching, which prevented practitioners from designing culturally responsive practices. How do you design culturally responsive practices if you lack knowledge of culturally responsive teaching? You can't, that's why I have dedicated subsequent chapters to boost your understanding of culturally meaningful teaching, so you will know exactly what it is.

One reason I focused on lacking knowledge, among other problems, is that you can transform this problem yourself—overnight. You do not necessarily need the assistance of your administrators or other people in your building to transform the problem. Through agency, you become competent at designing culturally meaningful practices (see Chapter 1 for a discussion on agency). You need to know a few things about the practice, and you need specific tools to guide you through the design process. If you are justice-oriented and willing to critique and problematize your practices, you may be ready to re-imagine your practices after reading just a few chapters.

In this chapter, I summarize the letter *L* of *The LEARN Framework*, which stands for learn. I lay out what you must learn and do to design culturally meaningful practices. By the end of this chapter, you will be able to:

- recognize why the letter *L—learn*—is step one in the framework and the design process;
- list *The Big Four*—four things you must learn to design culturally meaningful practices intentionally and purposefully; and
- articulate why it is impossible to design culturally meaningful practices intentionally without having knowledge of *The Big Four*.

Why do you think *learn* is the first component of *The LEARN Framework*? The first component is *Learn* because, historically, institutions have ignored the lived experiences, community practices, and cultural values of people of color. Institutions, scholars, and scholarship deemed people of color inferior and deficient to White people and mainstream culture. Teacher training programs did not—and some still do not—include the histories and contributions of culturally diverse learners when preparing for the teaching profession.

Therefore, we must learn about culturally responsive teaching, the contributions culturally diverse people have made to society, and our students' cultures, lived experiences, and community practices. If we don't know our students' cultures and cultural values, and if we lack knowledge of how culture affects teaching, learning, relationships, and engagement, it will be impossible to design culturally responsive practices intentionally and create equitable opportunities for all students in the classroom.

From this perspective, the letter *L, Learn*, is first because we cannot teach those we do not know; we cannot design something we do not understand. We must learn what culturally responsive teaching is, learn about our students' cultural values, and learn how to *design* culturally meaningful practices to create equitable opportunities for all. During the 7-week training, practitioners learned four specific things that helped them unpack culturally responsive teaching and design culturally responsive activities. I call these four things *The Big Four.*

The Big Four

Designing culturally responsive teaching requires you to learn certain things to develop culturally meaningful practices intentionally. In the space below, jot down things you need to know and be able to do to design culturally meaningful practices.

_____

_____

_____

_____

_____

_____

In what follows, I introduce four things you must know to design culturally responsive practices *intentionally* and sustain your practices over time. I call these *The Big Four.* These include knowing:

1. your why;
2. the history of culturally responsive education;
3. culturally responsive frameworks; and
4. cultural values and community practices.

Practitioners in my PhD research study commented that having knowledge of *The Big Four* was critical in helping them understand the importance of culturally responsive teaching. They explained that *The Big Four* effectively assisted them in designing culturally responsive activities. *The Big Four* gave them motivation, insight, and purpose for developing culturally responsive practices. Next, I briefly discuss each component of *The Big Four*.

1. Start with Why

When I train educators on culturally responsive teaching, they often request a quick-tip technical solution to boost engagement and develop relationships with students of color. For many teachers, culturally responsive teaching was about interventions. Teachers rarely reflected on why they should learn about culturally responsive teaching and design culturally responsive practices besides seeking technical solutions to boost engagement in the classroom. Culturally responsive teaching becomes more meaningful when we focus on our *why*.

Focusing on our *why* simply means reflecting on why we are engaging with culturally responsive teaching in the first place. It is reflecting on our purpose for learning about and designing culturally responsive practices. During my PhD study, all practitioners commented that reflecting on their why gave culturally responsive teaching deeper meaning than merely seeking interventions. Culturally responsive teaching requires us to learn about, reflect on, and challenge our why, which we will do in Chapter 7.

2. Historicity

The principle of historicity states—to understand a current problem, it is necessary to start with its history. When considering culturally responsive teaching, it is essential to know the history of culturally responsive education (CRE). History helps us understand how institutions and scholars blamed students of color for poor achievement and absolved racist systems that created inequity.

It is necessary to have historical knowledge of CRE to understand why scholars constructed culturally responsive teaching theories. When we start with history, we can assess the problem from its root and see how it evolved into the many challenges it presents today. For example, when we consider history, we understand that educating students of color in American schools is rooted in institutional racism. We learn that racist scholars produced racist scholarship. We discover that institutions required pre-service teachers to study this scholarship to prepare for the classroom. Because of this training, practitioners produce deficit-based thinking when working with students of color.

Some educators may subconsciously produce deficit-based thoughts about students of color and may be unaware that deficit-based thinking is rooted in racism. Culturally responsive teaching is the antidote to designing and implementing racist programming in school. After learning about *The Big Four*, you will see why.

When we do not consider history when addressing problems that prevent us from designing culturally responsive practices, we treat problems as if they were created yesterday or overnight. We act as if problems do not have a history, and we ignore that problems evolve. As I have highlighted, when educators learn about culturally responsive teaching, they often start by requesting technical solutions and interventions. When interventions fail, what do you suppose happens next? From my many years of experience, educators gave up. They were most concerned about interventions and less concerned about history. They stated something like, "Well, this culturally responsive stuff doesn't work," or "It's ineffective," or "I've tried . . ."

If you know the story of CRE, its history, development, and purpose, you will understand on a deeper level why culturally responsive teaching should be a regular part of everyday teaching and learning. As Gloria Ladson-Billings (1995) suggests, you will understand that culturally responsive teaching is just good teaching. It is quality instruction. It is not some add-on quick-tip, and it is not solely about interventions.

Practitioners in my study explained that learning to design culturally responsive practices became more personal and meaningful after learning about the history of CRE. They shared that understanding the history of culturally responsive teaching helped them identify their *why*—why they should learn about, design, and implement culturally responsive practices.

3. Culturally Responsive Frameworks

While working with colleagues or training educators in various states, practitioners often told me they were "doing culturally responsive teaching." When I asked, "What framework are you drawing from to design your practices?" they stated something like, "Framework? I don't use any frameworks. I just do what seems to work."

Culturally responsive teaching is applying theories and principles that comprise frameworks. If you are not drawing from a culturally responsive framework, you probably are doing something other than culturally responsive teaching. You are doing your own thing and calling it culturally responsive teaching. When you say you are doing culturally relevant, culturally responsive, culturally sustaining, or any other culturally meaningful work, you are saying you are drawing from a particular framework and applying principles associated with that framework in the classroom. Therefore, to design and implement culturally responsive practices *intentionally* and *purposefully*, you must understand culturally meaningful frameworks and their principles. I discuss this in Chapter 11 so you can avoid the tendency to do your own thing and call it "culturally responsive." Chapter 11 will help you become confident in defining culturally responsive teaching and describing what it is and what it is not.

4. Cultural Values and Community Practices

There are decades of research on cultural values that many people embrace across race, class, and culture. While it is stereotypical to conclude that individuals embrace cultural values based solely on race, understanding the research on cultural values will help us better understand mainstream values and how they show up in our instructional practices. This understanding also helps us become aware of cultural values that many students in general and students of color, in particular, may embrace.

Again, it is stereotypical to assume that students will embrace specific cultural values based on their skin color. Knowing cultural values will help you name and describe values that students across races may embrace and prefer over other values. Understanding cultural values is a great place to start with reflecting on your own cultural values and how your values may differ from your students' values. It is crucial to examine how differences in your cultural values and your students' values often clash in the classroom and shatter relationships. I discuss this in Chapters 9 and 10 so you can examine your cultural values and learn how to spot cultural clashes that create tension and shatter relationships.

Summary

The letter *L* of *The LEARN Framework* stands for learn. It refers to learning about what I call *The Big Four*—(1) your why; (2) the history of culturally responsive education; (3) culturally responsive frameworks; and (4) cultural values and community practices. Understanding *The Big Four* will ground you as you prepare to design culturally responsive practices. It is challenging to design culturally responsive practices *intentionally* without having knowledge of *The Big Four*.

What's Next?

In the next chapter, I unbox the letter *L* of *The LEARN Framework*. I start with discussing the importance of learning about your *why*—your purpose for action—when designing culturally responsive teaching. Your *why* will sustain you when you experience stuck points and other challenges with culturally meaningful teaching.

Chapter 6:

L—Learn: Start with Why

———— ❦ ————

Every single organization on the planet knows what they do. Some know how they do it. Very few know why they do it.

—Simon Sinek

When I train educators on culturally responsive teaching, they all say the same thing. They say, "Dwayne, I love your work. I love the concept of culturally responsive trauma-informed support. I love the idea of integrating hip-hop, R&B, and Reggaeton with SEL programming, but where do I start?"

My question to you is, where should we start? In the space below, take a moment to jot down where we should start when designing culturally meaningful practices.

_____

_____

_____

_____

In this chapter, I discuss the importance of identifying and reflecting on your why when designing culturally meaningful practices. By the end of this chapter, you will:

- recognize the benefits of identifying your why when designing culturally meaningful practices; and
- reflect on your why to prepare for the design process.

Simon Sinek, a bestselling author and inspirational speaker, would say we should start by reflecting on our *why*. Before becoming an inspirational speaker, Simon owned a successful business. Although his company did well financially, he lost all interest in the business and no longer cared about providing his services. He regained passion for and interest in his business after reflecting on *why* he started the business. Because of this experience, from reflecting on his why, Simon had an epiphany that changed his life.

He created a visual of his epiphany that includes three concentric circles. In the outer circle, he includes the word *what*. He includes the word *how* in the next circle, and within the inner circle, he includes the word *why*. Figure 4 illustrates his epiphany.

Figure 4: Start with Why

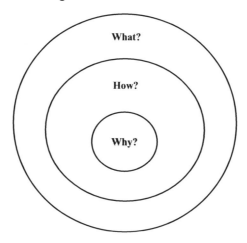

Simon calls this the *Golden Circle*, and he uses it to describe his job experiences. He explained that he knew *what* he was doing within his business before losing passion; he knew *how* to run the business successfully. However, over time, he lost sight of *why* he got into business. He lost sight of the underlying reason he provided services for others. After reflecting on his why, he regained passion for his work and business. After reflecting on his experiences, he became even more passionate about his work.

Simon now travels the country and talks to organizations about starting with why when considering their purpose, work, and other areas of life. Based on this epiphany, Simon argues that organizations know exactly *what* they do. Some, he says, know *how* they do it. But very few individuals and organizations reflect on *why* they do what they do; he says that very few individuals within organizations focus on their why. Your why does not refer to earning a wage. Instead, why refers to your purpose; it relates to your beliefs about why you should do a particular thing.

Although Simon Sinek is not a K-12 or post-secondary educator, his epiphany and principles relate to culturally responsive teaching and culturally responsive training. For example, most people who consider culturally responsive teaching know what it is (they know that it pertains to culture, teaching, and students); some know how to do it; however, very few I have trained focused on their why. What's your why? Reflect on your why by thinking about this question: Do you believe educators should implement culturally responsive practices? After reflecting on this "yes, no, maybe so-kind of question," reflect on why you think you should or should not implement culturally responsive practices throughout the day.

This activity is about whether you believe we should implement culturally responsive practices or not. That's it. You might respond yes and then explain why you think we should. You might respond no–that implementing culturally responsive teaching is unnecessary. If your response is no, reflect on why you believe it is unnecessary.

There is no right or wrong answer. You are simply reflecting on your why. When I give you the signal, jot down your why on the *Start with Why* workspace below. Spend sufficient time identifying your why because I have a special activity for you in the next chapter. But to complete the special activity, you must document your why in this section. Are you ready to write about your why? Let's do that now.

Start with Why Workspace:

Remember there is no right or wrong answer to your why. The activity is a self-awareness activity, allowing you to reflect on your beliefs regarding culturally responsive teaching. We will follow up on this activity in the next section.

Summary

In this chapter, I discussed the author and inspirational speaker Simon Sinek's concept of starting with why. As part of the *L* component of *The LEARN Framework*, I shared that learning about and reflecting on your why is vital. By the end of my PhD research study, all practitioners identified their why. They commented that their *why* grounded them in the work.

What's Next?

In the next chapter, I discuss the importance of learning about and understanding the history of culturally responsive education (CRE) when unpacking culturally responsive teaching and designing culturally responsive practices. I will conclude the chapter with the special activity I mentioned earlier. You are in for a treat. By using *The LEARN Framework*, I guarantee you will learn how to implement culturally responsive practices. I guarantee it, and since I am confident in the framework, I am super pumped for this book section and to learn how you respond to the following few chapters and activities. Prepare to get your hands dirty. Prepare to reject specific theories oppressive to Black and Brown students. Prepare to challenge your why.

Chapter 7:

L — Learn: The History of Culturally Responsive Education

———— ∞ ————

> . . . But I think it's just also like, understanding the history is the why to it . . . it's like, why do we need to do this work? And, and I think understanding, also that, like, although [culturally responsive teaching] may feel new to some of us, it's not that new. And there's actually lots of years of research behind it. And so it's just important that we're able to explain, in this group and to others, like the history of it, and why we need to do this and why it's best practice for our students. So I think the history kind of helps explain the why.
>
> **—PhD Research Participant**

D o you think it is necessary to know and understand the history of culturally responsive teaching? What does history do for us when learning about culturally responsive education (CRE) and designing culturally responsive practices? In the space below, jot down your thoughts about this question: Is it important to understand the history of culturally responsive teaching when designing culturally responsive practices?

Is it Necessary to Understand the History of CRE? Explain Your Thoughts.

In this chapter, we will learn about the history of CRE. By the end of this chapter, you will be able to:

- articulate why understanding the history of CRE grounds you when designing culturally meaningful practices;
- describe why culturally meaningful teaching is a mindset rooted in assumptions and beliefs; and
- reconsider your why, using the history of CRE to guide your thinking.

Educators in my PhD study commented that understanding the history of CRE was the most important learning activity that helped them identify their why. After you learn about the history of CRE, I want you to return to your why; reconsider your why. By the end of the chapter, determine if you shifted your why or if your why stayed the same. Let's dive into the history!

The War on Poverty

On January 8, 1964, President Lyndon B. Johnson and his administration declared war on poverty. President Johnson said, to eradicate and prevent poverty in America, every American citizen must have increased opportunities and that all students, including students of color, must achieve in the classroom.

From this declaration, the academic achievement of students in America became a political issue, for Americans could not eradicate poverty if they could not read, write, compute, or problem-solve using numbers. The war on poverty immediately shed light on students who underachieved in the classroom; specifically, the war shed light on students of color and students from impoverished backgrounds. The question of the time was, why do students of color and students from low socioeconomic backgrounds perform poorly in the classroom?

1960s Theories

During the 1960s, scholars proposed answers. They argued that students of color and students from impoverished communities underachieved because of genetic deficiencies. They believed that their poor performance was a direct reflection of genetic inferiority. From this view, scholars argued that students of color and those from low-income backgrounds could never achieve academically because they were genetically incapable of processing information and learning at high levels. It was clear from their perspectives—and scholarship supported this theory—that their poor performance was a symptom of flawed genes.

Scholarship contended that students of color and those from impoverished backgrounds were destined to fail in the classroom. Scholars argued there was nothing anyone could do to correct this predisposition to failure. From this perspective, their performance revealed their true abilities. According to this view, although students of color were underachieving compared to their White counterparts, they performed at their potential, consistent with their skills and genetic makeup. These explanations blamed students of color and students from low-income communities for academic failures and ignored inequity and racist practices and policies prevalent in schools.

1970s Theories

During the 1970s, however, scholars rejected genetic deficit theories. They argued that students of color and those from low-income backgrounds were not genetically deficient. Instead of explaining poor performance on inferior genes, these scholars were more liberal. Consistent with their liberal views, they attributed poor performance to students' cultures.

From this view, they argued that students of color and students from low-income communities were culturally deficient, making them culturally inferior to White people in particular and White students in general. They believed that students underachieved because they lacked cultural resources. They argued that students of color had no books, magazines, or newspapers in the home to read and that these youngsters had no fathers in the house to learn from.

Although students of color and students from low-income backgrounds came to school with rich languages and ways of sharing knowledge, scholars described their language as poor English. They contended that students spoke poorly because their mothers did not interact with them at home. Some scholars described Black mothers as lazy, loud, bossy, and sexually promiscuous. They used these characteristics to explain the underachievement of students of color and students from low-income backgrounds.

Deficit-Based Theories

Genetic and cultural deficiency theories are deficit theories, which contend that students of color underperform in the classroom because they lack something within their homes, communities, cultures, minds, or bodies. A major problem with deficit-based theories was that they blamed students, their genetic makeup, their communities, their cultures, and their parents for poor outcomes. While blaming students for their own miseducation, they ignored racist policies that governed behaviors in schools and inequitable practices taking place in the classroom. A popular intervention was to force students of color to learn and behave according to Eurocentric values and standards and to teach them to reject their own languages, literacies, and community practices considering their languages, cultures, and community practices led to academic underachievement.

1970s and 1980s Theories

During the 1970s and 1980s, antiracist scholars rebutted deficit-thinking theories. They postulated cultural difference theories, contending that students of color and students from low socioeconomic backgrounds were not culturally deficient but came from cultures that differed from mainstream culture. Cultural difference scholarship argued that schools contributed to the underachievement of students of color by ignoring the cultural values, assets, and literacies students brought to school.

Scholars maintained that, instead of seeking to assimilate students of color to Eurocentric values, school leaders should use students' cultures and ways of being as bridges to teach in the classroom. Although culturally different scholars argued for mixing students' cultural values with instruction and provided research that articulated the need to integrate cultural values within the classroom, they did not offer culturally meaningful teaching pedagogies that educators could employ to enhance academic outcomes.

1990s and 2000s Theories

During the 1990s and 2000s, scholars conducted studies rooted in cultural difference scholarship and devised culturally responsive teaching theories. Culturally responsive teaching theories—also known as culturally responsive pedagogies—contend that many students of color experience cultural clashes in the classroom, indicating that their home and community cultures are dissimilar to the school culture, contributing to their poor performance. Culturally responsive teaching theories are frameworks that guide educators through mixing the cultural values, community practices, and lived experiences of students with instruction. *Culturally responsive teaching* is an umbrella term that describes an array of practices that integrate the cultures and literacies of students with instruction. The belief then, when seeking to design culturally responsive practices, is:

1. all students come from rich cultural backgrounds;
2. culturally responsive practices can prepare students of color to process their lived experiences, including experiences related to racial violence, injustice, and discrimination; and
3. the school curriculum should include students' cultural values, lived experiences, and community practices, instead of excluding these practices because of deficit-based beliefs.

Now that you've learned about the history, including why scholars constructed culturally responsive practices, let's revisit your why. I'll ask the same question I asked in the previous chapter: Do you believe educators should implement culturally responsive practices? After revisiting this question, reflect on why you think we should or should not implement culturally responsive practices throughout the day. As you reflect on this question, determine if you shifted your why in significant ways, if your why stayed the same, or if you've made minor changes to your why.

Reconsidering Your Why:

Now that you've read about the history, reconsider the question at the start of this chapter:

Is it important to know about the history of culturally responsive education?

_____

_____

_____

_____

_____

_____

_____

_____

_____

_____

_____

Did you change your response to this question now that you understand the history of culturally responsive education, or did you have the same answer? Reflect on your two responses, and why you may hold the views you do about understanding the history of CRE when designing culturally meaningful practices.

Summary

In this chapter, I discussed the history of CRE, starting with The War on Poverty. Scholars constructed theories to explain the underachievement of students of color and students from low-income backgrounds. Scholars during the 1960s constructed genetic deficiency theories to explain the underachievement of students, and scholars during the 1970s articulated cultural deficiency theories. During the 1990s, scholars rebutted deficit-based ideas and constructed cultural difference theories. Scholars during the 2000s conducted studies on cultural difference theories, and they published culturally responsive teaching theories from their research.

What's Next?

In the next chapter, I discuss three culturally meaningful teaching frameworks you can use when designing culturally meaningful practices. During the design process, practitioners used these frameworks as a guide to design culturally responsive SEL activities. In the next chapter, you will learn about these three frameworks and why it is impossible to design culturally meaningful practices *intentionally* without knowledge of culturally responsive teaching frameworks.

Chapter 8:

L—Learn: Culturally Responsive Frameworks

———— ✖ ————

So I originally went with the culturally relevant pedagogy and kind of did all of you know, filled out how am I helping them achieve this. And then I really got stuck with number three [critical consciousness]. And Dwayne and I talked a little bit and it's really like, because it's such a structured curriculum . . . I wasn't like sure how to do this. And then it made me think that maybe I picked the wrong framework . . . I'm using the surveys [for] the opening activities . . . I did not have a focus group at first, but then as I was rereading to kind of better understand some of the principles, I went back and added the focus group. And then also the individual interviews up here because when I was thinking about it, too, like when I work with these students, I find out that there is a lot of students who identify as gay or a different area, and I don't always know right away unless it comes up in conversation or [the] teacher shared with me. So, like really being able to have this information beforehand [data collected from a tool practitioners designed]. So I went back and added that, [to describe] how they will experience academic success.

—PhD Research Participant

D o you provide culturally meaningful practices in your area of work? If your response is yes, my next question is—What framework do you use to guide your practices? In the space below, provide the names of culturally meaningful frameworks you use to guide your instructional activities. If you have never designed culturally meaningful practices or applied culturally meaningful frameworks, provide the name(s) of culturally meaningful frameworks with which you are familiar. If you are unfamiliar with culturally meaningful frameworks, simply put question marks in the space below. No worries if you cannot recall any frameworks. You'll be able to recall at least three by the end of this chapter.

Culturally Meaningful Frameworks You Know:

1._____

2._____

3._____

4._____

5._____

In this chapter, I will introduce three prominent scholars who influenced the field of culturally responsive education (CRE), scholars you should know if you are designing culturally meaningful activities. I will share their respective frameworks, definitions of culturally responsive teaching, and essential principles that comprise their frameworks. You should take notes in this chapter because, in Chapter 11, I will teach you how to apply these frameworks and principles in the classroom. By the end of this chapter, you will be able to:

- recognize three prominent scholars in the field of culturally meaningful teaching;
- identify three frameworks you can use as a guide to design culturally meaningful activities, just as practitioners did in my PhD study; and
- recognize essential principles that comprise each framework.

I've said it a few times throughout this book, and I will repeat it because it's just that important. Designing culturally meaningful practices *intentionally* is challenging, if not impossible, if you lack knowledge of culturally meaningful frameworks and principles. In this chapter, you will learn why.

Culturally Meaningful Frameworks

When considering culturally meaningful frameworks, including the three prominent ones I will share in this chapter, view them as theories that build upon previous theories. Instead of viewing culturally meaningful frameworks as separate, distinct, and opposing theories, know that scholars have incorporated previous theories into their work. Although some frameworks may incorporate different principles, they all have the same core goal. That goal is to pair students' cultural values, community practices, and lived experiences with instruction.

In what follows, I discuss the work of Gloria Ladson-Billings, who coined culturally relevant pedagogy, Geneva Gay, who addresses culturally responsive teaching, and Django Paris, who coined culturally sustaining pedagogy. When people say they are implementing "culturally responsive teaching" practices, there is a good chance they are referring to one of these frameworks. So, let's take a deep dive and understand what these scholars mean when they argue for culturally responsive teaching!

Three Prominent Scholars

Gloria Ladson-Billings—Culturally Relevant Pedagogy

What is culturally *relevant* teaching? What do these terms mean, and how did Gloria Ladson-Billings know what to call and include in her culturally relevant pedagogy framework? Gloria Ladson-Billings' framework (1995) emerged from the work of scholars who preceded her, in addition to the findings of her research, in which she spent 3 years studying teachers who successfully engaged African American students in the classroom. During her research, deficit-based theories dominated education literature; scholars articulated their opinions of what was wrong with students of color and students from impoverished backgrounds that prevented them from learning at a high level.

Instead of relying on deficit-based thinking and searching for what was wrong with African American students based on Anglo cultural values, Ladson-Billings sought what was right with African American students. She did this by studying the teaching practices of eight elementary school teachers who successfully engaged African American students in the classroom. All eight teachers placed the cultural values, community practices, and lived experiences of African American students at the center of instruction (Ladson-Billings, 1995). They all used students' values to drive instruction. Rather than relying on prepackaged programs or prescriptive curricula, teachers designed culturally relevant activities in their own way.

Ladson-Billings (1995) stated that it was a nightmare studying teachers' practices because they all did their own thing, using their students' cultural values, community practices, and lived experiences. This is significant because it shows that your practices may not look like mine or your colleagues' when you design culturally meaningful practices. Do you know why this is the case? The answer is that your practices will be a combination of your students' interests, your knowledge, your skill set, your beliefs, your assumptions, and your motivation for designing the activity. Ideally, your practices will be a combination of your values *and* your students' values. There is no cookie-cutter approach when designing culturally meaningful activities. Activities should combine your students' cultural interests and your knowledge, skills, and abilities.

Ladson-Billings' Findings

Table 1 includes Ladson-Billings' (1995) definition of culturally relevant teaching, her framework name, and the guiding principles that comprise her framework.

Table 1: Culturally Relevant Pedagogy Framework—Gloria Ladson-Billings

Definition	Framework Name	Guiding Principles
"A pedagogy of opposition, not unlike critical pedagogy, but specifically committed to the collective, not merely individual empowerment" (Ladson-Billings, 1995, p. 160).	Culturally Relevant Pedagogy	1. Students will experience academic success. 2. Students will develop/maintain cultural competence and academic excellence. 3. Students will develop a critical consciousness through which they challenge the status quo and current social order (pp. 160-162)

After studying teachers' practices for 3 years and analyzing how they engaged students of color and students from impoverished backgrounds, Ladson-Billings identified three essential components of their practices. These three practices make up her culturally relevant framework. From studying their practices, Ladson-Billings found that teachers successful at engaging students did at least three important things exceptionally well:

Principle #1: *Academic Success*

Despite what was happening in society at the time and in students' lives, teachers expected all students to thrive in the classroom. This was the expectation. All teachers in Ladson-Billings' study created opportunities for students to experience *academic success.*

Principle #2: *Cultural Competence*

You might wonder how teachers in Ladson-Billings' study achieved academic success with all students. The answer is teachers placed their students' cultural values, community practices, and lived experiences at the center of instruction; they used their students' strengths and cultural interests to drive instruction. For example, one White teacher noticed that her Black boys possessed social power and had an unusual ability to influence their peers. The boys were charismatic leaders; they could get others to follow their lead.

Instead of allowing the boys to lead their peers in the wrong direction in her classroom, the teacher created opportunities for the boys to take on academic leadership roles during instructional time. The boys used their gifts, talents, abilities, cultural values, and swag to engage other students in the classroom. They learned about their own cultural values and social identities while learning how to become successful in the classroom, using their social identities to inspire others.

Because of the boys' leadership, other students became academic leaders. Notice that the teacher did not allow the boys' social power to disrupt the classroom, and she did not allow them to make a mockery of her instruction. Instead, she created opportunities to develop their leadership skills in the classroom and taught them how to inspire others academically. This principle, *cultural competence*, is about cultivating cultural integrity in the classroom. Cultural integrity refers to respecting and celebrating cultural values, traditions, customs, heritage, and practices.

Principle #3: *Critical Consciousness*

According to Ladson-Billings (1995), culturally relevant teaching is not only about ensuring *academic success* and developing *cultural competence* among students of color; it is also a process of creating opportunities for students to develop *critical consciousness.* She defines critical consciousness as conscious awareness and the ability to " . . . critique the cultural norms, values, mores, and institutions that produce and maintain social inequities" (p. 162). Critical consciousness is critically engaging the world and others; it is perceiving the world through a critical lens by critiquing dominant narratives and systems within society. Critical consciousness is also known as sociopolitical consciousness (p. 162), in which students challenge the status quo and societal problems, including issues related to injustice, racism, and discrimination.

Geneva Gay—Culturally Responsive Teaching

The second prominent scholar I will introduce is Geneva Gay. Whereas Gloria Ladson-Billings uses the term *culturally relevant pedagogy* to describe the essence of her framework, Geneva Gay prefers the term *culturally responsive teaching.* In her book, *Culturally Responsive Teaching* (2018), Gay lets us know that she borrows concepts from various scholars to construct her culturally responsive framework. In what follows, I share how Gay defines culturally responsive teaching and the four principles of her framework.

Culturally Responsive Teaching Definition

Table 2 includes Gay's (2014) definition of culturally responsive teaching, her framework name, and the guiding principles that comprise her framework.

Table 2: Culturally Responsive Teaching Framework—Geneva Gay

Definition	Framework Name	Guiding Principles
"Culturally responsive teaching uses the cultural orientations, heritages, and background experiences of students of color as referents and resources to improve their school achievement" (Gay, 2014, p. 357).	Culturally Responsive Teaching	1. A need to teach to and through students. 2. A need to build bridges for teachers and students to cross. 3. Race, ethnicity, and culture matter profoundly in teaching and learning. 4. Changing perceptions of underachieving students from *problems* to *possibilities.* (Gay, 2014, pp. 357-359)

Gay (2014) contends that "culturally responsive teaching uses the cultural orientations, heritages, and background experiences of students of color as referents and resources to improve their school achievement" (p. 357). According to Gay, four principles guide culturally responsive teaching. She says culturally responsive teaching is a process of "teaching *to* and *through*" (p. 357) ethnic, racial, and cultural diversity. Teaching *to* students refers to teaching students of all races about the cultures, experiences, challenges, and accomplishments of racially and ethnically diverse learners. Teaching *through* students refers to using the cultural knowledge of ethnically diverse learners when teaching them instructional content and developing skills.

The second principle is building bridges for students and teachers to cross cultural borders. Building bridges helps students become culturally proficient in multiple cultural settings. This includes creating opportunities for students to become knowledgeable about and aware of their culture *and* mainstream culture, including school culture. The essence of building bridges is inclusive education instead of subtractive education.

Inclusive education embraces and supports indigenous languages, cultural values, community practices, and cultural diversity. Subtractive education seeks to take away from students. Students must assimilate to mainstream culture to the extent that they lose parts of themselves, including aspects of their language, cultures, and community practices.

The third guiding principle argues that race, ethnicity, and culture are inherent features of humanity and US society and therefore matter in teaching and learning. I will share two examples to illustrate the importance of race, ethnicity, and culture and their impact on education. During the pandemic, a school district I provided consultation services for invited students back into the building to learn inside of the classroom. They were transitioning students from remote learning back into the building. To assist in this transitioning process, one counselor contacted the parents on her caseload to invite students back into the building. One of her students struggled with remote learning, so the counselor attempted to get the student back into the building quickly to provide additional learning support.

The student's mother told the counselor she was considering whether she would allow her child to return; she was unsure of her decision. After weeks of attempting to get the student in the building, the counselor recommended that I contact the parent. I contacted the parent to check on the student. Upon hearing my voice, the parent stated, "I do not plan to send my child back because I believe the leaders in that building are inviting Black students and other students of color back into the building. The parent demonstrated a different attitude and tone when she spoke with me. She said, "I'm not going to let y'all experiment with my child." Although it was my first time talking with the parent, she spoke with me as if we had known each other for years. We had a pleasant, long conversation, but the conversation that she had with me was drastically different from the conversation she had with the White counselor.

When the parent heard my voice, it was evident that she made the connection that I was a Black male; she even identified me as a Black male. I eventually shared this experience and the parent's concern with the counselor. After learning this, the counselor commented that the parent had never brought up race-related issues with her. From this experience, I discussed Gay's (2014) culturally responsive teaching principle with the counselor—that race matters in education.

Another example is, considering I am a Black male, students of color may interpret and process lessons on race and racism differently from how they would if a White male were to introduce a lesson on race and racism. Students might question the White teacher's intentions of sharing the lesson or wonder how the White teacher feels about people of color in general and Black people in particular. These examples show that race, ethnicity, and culture matter profoundly in teaching and learning.

The fourth guiding principle is shifting the narrative of students of color from *problems* to *possibilities*. This principle is rooted in history in that, historically, scholars identified marginalized students as problems to be fixed, which was rooted in deficit-based thinking; culturally responsive teaching principles provide counter-narratives by focusing on students' assets, including their cultural values, community practices, gifts, talents, and abilities.

Django Paris—Culturally Sustaining Pedagogy

The third prominent scholar I will introduce is Django Paris. Whereas Gloria Ladson-Billings uses the term *culturally relevant pedagogy* and Geneva Gay uses the term *culturally responsive teaching,* Django Paris uses the term *culturally sustaining pedagogy* to describe the essence of his work. Table 3 includes Paris's (2012) definition of culturally sustaining teaching, his framework name, and the guiding principles that comprise his framework.

Table 3: Culturally Sustaining Pedagogy—Django Paris

Definition	Framework Name	Guiding Principles
A pedagogy that "seeks to perpetuate and foster—to sustain—linguistic, literate, and cultural pluralism as part of the democratic project of schooling" (Paris, 2012, p. 93).	Culturally Sustaining Pedagogy	1. A focus on the plural and evolving nature of **youth identity** and **cultural practices** and a commitment to embracing youth culture's counter-hegemonic potential; 2. While maintaining a clear-eyed critique of how youth culture can also reproduce systemic inequalities. (Paris & Alim, 2014, p. 85)

Culturally sustaining pedagogy builds on the body of scholarship related to culturally responsive teaching. According to Paris (2012), culturally sustaining pedagogy "seeks to perpetuate and foster—to sustain—linguistic, literate, and cultural pluralism as part of the democratic project of schooling" (p. 93).

He contends that, while policies and practices seek to create a monocultural and monolingual society, culturally sustaining pedagogy aims to develop cultural pluralism. Paris (2012) provided a "loving critique" of culturally responsive pedagogies, including culturally relevant pedagogy (Ladson-Billings, 1995) and culturally responsive teaching (Gay, 2014). He questioned whether terms such as "relevant" and "responsive" were sufficient for capturing the goal of creating bi-and multiculturalism and whether they were sufficient for sustaining the heritage ways of being and community practices of culturally diverse learners (Paris, 2012, p. 93). Paris commented that not only should instruction be relevant and responsive to the experiences of students, but that instruction should seek to sustain the languages and literacies through culturally meaningful practices. When seeking to understand what culturally meaningful practices mean, refer to the framework; review the culturally sustaining table and focus on the definition and guiding principles.

Paris (2012) says that instead of "using" the cultural practices of students to learn the "acceptable curricular canon" that is taught in schools, instruction should seek to sustain the languages, heritages, and identities of students (Paris, 2012, p. 95). In addition to community practices, culturally sustaining pedagogies emphasize youth culture, including hip-hop cultural elements. Paris and Alim (2017) contend that hip-hop pedagogy "is an organic form of CSP [culturally sustaining practice]" (p. 159). They provide three reasons integrating hip-hop with instruction is an example of CSP.

First, they contend that hip-hop emphasizes "knowledge of self" as a political, self-conscious awareness pedagogical activity (p. 159). As a conscious activity, hip-hop artists raise awareness around sociopolitical experiences that occurred in their childhood communities and experiences that happen throughout the country; artists shed light on how these experiences developed their identities and influenced their actions in society.

Second, hip-hop espouses the practice of sampling, the process of "archiving" and "reviving" cultural traditions (Alim & Haupt, 2017, p. 159). From this view, hip-hop draws from historical experiences by sampling and remixing music (Seidel, Simmons, and Lipset, 2022) in ways that reflect contemporary concerns. Third and finally, practitioners and pedagogical theorists who integrate hip-hop elements in the classroom with instruction organically "sustain and revive the souls of students who, for too often, experience schooling as a soul-deadening process where the very things that they hold dear—their languages, cultures, families, identities, and histories—are absent, stigmatized, marginalized, and excluded" (Alim & Haupt, 2017, p. 159).

In previous chapters, I made the claim it is challenging, if not impossible, to design culturally meaningful practices *intentionally* without having knowledge of culturally meaningful frameworks. The reason is that culturally meaningful teaching is *applying* culturally meaningful techniques and principles. If you don't know of these frameworks and principles, it will be impossible to design culturally meaningful practices in intentional ways.

Summary

In this chapter, I discussed the work of three prominent scholars who write about culturally responsive teaching, including Gloria Ladson-Billings, Geneva Gay, and Django Paris. I shared how they define culturally responsive teaching, I discussed their frameworks, and I included principles that shape their frameworks. Although I shared three frameworks in this chapter, there are an array of culturally responsive teaching frameworks that comprise culturally responsive education (CRE). Culturally responsive teaching is applying culturally responsive principles and frameworks in intentional and meaningful ways.

What's Next?

In the next chapter, I discuss cultural values and community practices. I show their relevance to CRE so you will know why it is critical to place students' cultural values and practices at the center of instruction.

Chapter 9:

L—Learn: Cultural Values and Community Practices

Yeah, I don't think there's a right or wrong on this. But I think for this one, I would probably go with culturally relevant pedagogy. Even in thinking about designing a community building activity, I would want to know, like, I mean, again, to make sure that I don't equate race and culture to start figuring out like, who are these students? What values do they have for themselves . . . but also, like, once I get an understanding of what their cultural values are then being able to develop something from there, right? Because thinking about the definition of empowering students intellectually, socially, emotionally, and politically, using their cultural references to impart that knowledge. So, if I'm trying to teach SEL skills, and I'm thinking about, you know, those five SEL skills, I already know the knowledge that I want them to have [SEL], or the outcome. So now thinking about, okay, what references [students' cultural values, community practices, and lived experiences] can I use to help teach those skills?

—PhD Research Participant

W hen you hear the word cultural values, what comes to your mind? How do you define this phrase? How do you define community practices? Use the space below to define cultural values and community practices, then write at least five cultural values with which you are familiar. No worries if you cannot explain these terms or think of examples. By the end of this chapter, you'll understand cultural values and community practices, and you will be able to provide examples of both.

Define Cultural Values and Community Practices:

Cultural values are

_____

_____

_____

_____

Community practices are

_____

_____

_____

_____

List Cultural Values That You Can Recall:

1._____

2._____

3._____

4._____

5._____

When I train educators on culturally responsive teaching, they seem to favor content related to cultural values and community practices over other content. Seeing them lean forward while taking notes on every word that pertains to cultural values is interesting. I provided a keynote talk in Florida, discussing cultural values and community practices. At the end of the training, an administrator requested that I train her district on the content. She stated that she was about to leave the conference before I spoke, but when I introduced cultural values and illustrated them using music and short video clips, the information snatched her attention. She stayed and took notes to share with her teams.

Throughout this book, I have shared that it would be challenging to design culturally responsive practices in intentional ways if we are unfamiliar with culturally responsive frameworks. It would be equally challenging, if not impossible, to design culturally responsive practices if we are unfamiliar with our students' cultural values and community practices. It would be difficult because culturally meaningful practices require that we center their values, practices, experiences, and literacies in the classroom.

In this chapter, I will share eight cultural values that inspire my work as an equity coach and school-based practitioner. By the end of this chapter, you will be able to:

- debunk a pervasive myth related to race and culture that prevents educators from designing culturally meaningful practices;
- recognize five cultural values associated with traditional African American culture;
- recognize three cultural values associated with mainstream culture; and
- understand why we should consider historical events when exploring students' cultural interests instead of assuming that students embrace specific values based on race.

When co-designing culturally responsive practices with students, I am conscious of the eight cultural values I will introduce in this chapter. I use them to describe my students' experiences if their experiences are related to the values. However, before sharing this information with practitioners, I always address myths about race and culture, so educators do not haphazardly design activities based on race and "cultural values" rather than their students' cultural histories and experiences.

Myths Related to Race and Culture

What false assumptions about race and culture are holding you back from designing culturally meaningful practices, assumptions that make you feel you can never become competent at designing culturally responsive activities? We do not have to become experts on culture, race, or culturally responsive teaching. It is critically important, however, that we become knowledgeable about and debunk common myths related to race and culture, so we do not engage in prejudicial and stereotypical practices while designing "culturally responsive activities." When I train educators on myths related to race and culture, I typically address three common myths. However, in this book, I address a common myth that educators commonly embrace; it is a false assumption that some educators draw from when designing culturally responsive practices for students of color.

Race and Culture Are Not Synonymous

The myth we must debunk before discussing cultural values and community practices is the false assumption that race and culture are synonymous. This is not only a myth, but this belief is pervasive in schools, and teachers design activities based on their students' race rather than their culture. Here is how they do it. Since they believe race and culture are synonymous, they think that students value certain things based solely on race.

I have coached educators who designed activities for Black students based on stereotypes rather than their students' cultural values and histories. This happened when teachers believed that Black students were communal, valued working in groups, embraced hip-hop, and were "vervistic" (a term you will learn later in this chapter). Based on these stereotypes, they placed Black students in cooperative learning groups often, paired hip-hop with instruction, then called this culturally responsive teaching.

Although many Black students are communal, prefer working in groups, and embrace hip-hop, other Black students may not embrace these values and practices. Just because a student is Black does not mean she will value some "Black culture." Similarly, just because a student is White does not mean he will respond favorably to traditional Eurocentric or mainstream values, and the same goes for all other racial and cultural group members.

I like what Boykin and Noguera (2011) say in their book, *Creating the Opportunity to Learn*. They remind us that we cannot tell the cultural book by the racial cover. I read this book in 2011, the year it was published, and that quote has stuck with me ever since. That is, we cannot tell the cultural book by the racial cover. We cannot predict what students will value based on their skin color.

Instead, we must create opportunities for students to showcase their cultural histories, values, and interests, and then use their experiences to inform instruction in the classroom across tiers. Notice that creating opportunities for students to share their cultural histories and using their values to inform instruction is in stark contrast to employing quick-tip solutions or designing activities based on assumptions about race, culture, and values.

Having this knowledge is a prerequisite to designing culturally responsive practices. It helps us understand that we engage in stereotypical behaviors by attempting to include things in our lessons based simply on what we believe about our students' racial groups without understanding their cultural values and histories. Engaging in such behaviors contrasts with culturally responsive teaching. It is contradictory; we cannot be culturally responsive *and* design lessons based on stereotypes. Doing this puts us at risk of harming culturally diverse learners, shattering relationships with them, and making them believe we are racist educators. Instead of designing culturally meaningful practices, we create disharmony and racial tension in the classroom and call these practices culturally responsive.

When educators believe that race and culture are synonymous, they assume that Black students come from pre-packaged, pre-formed, ready-made cultures—that when Black people are conceived into this world, they enter with pre-established values. For example, it is common to believe that Black students come from cultures that embrace movement, music, rap, and entertainment—and the belief is that students require these things to do well in the classroom. This is a stereotypical assumption.

I have collaborated with teachers who attempted to design culturally responsive activities for Black students. They sought to include activities related to movement, dance, rap, and other cultural values, thinking Black students desired those activities. Rather than exploring their students' cultural histories, these educators designed solely based on assumptions. I know educators who also attempted to design activities based on cultural values without seeking to understand if said cultural values were a part of their students' historical experiences.

When I train educators, I discuss cultural values because they are critical to culturally meaningful teaching. However, instead of designing activities based on assumptions about race and culture, I subscribe to creating lessons based on the *histories* of students. This means identifying historical *events* and *activities* that students experienced throughout their development and understanding the *tools* (resources) they used to engage with the activities. I'll define events, activities, and tools to make this idea more concrete.

I define *events* as students' lived experiences; an event is an experience—an encounter in life. Being born into this world is an event; each interaction with a family member is an event; each interaction with teachers and peers at school is an event; racist interactions are events. We experience a host of events throughout our development. These events become meaningful to us, and we use them to predict, interpret, and navigate the world. Events shape our identities.

I define *activities* as community practices students participate in within their homes and communities. Activities include household practices that family members participate in during family reunions and get-togethers. The goal is to identify those activities—home and community practices—that students value. This could indeed be dancing, rapping, drawing, singing, and other practices we might associate with specific races. However, the key is not to design based on preconceived notions about race and culture. We must avoid planning activities based on stereotypes.

When we design based on the histories of our students—instead of their races— we design based on their lived experiences with events, activities, and tools rather than on notions that race and culture are synonymous. When identifying histories, students learn that they have similar experiences as others who are not a part of their racial group and find common cultural values with their teachers and peers.

Finally, I define *tools* as artifacts individuals use to make activities happen. For example, if a student embraces drawing, he may be interested in materials that create opportunities for him to draw. He may desire writing utensils and sketch pads. Suppose a student values rapping as a cultural and community practice. There, she may be interested in listening to music, writing lyrics, and being creative with words. She may desire tools such as headphones, AirPods, phones, and other devices to engage lyrically.

Now get this. If students embrace communalism and community, we could use this value as a tool in the classroom by engaging in meaningful group work. Again, to do this, we would have to know our students' values and not design practices based on assumptions and myths related to race and culture. Therefore, instead of creating activities based on the myth that race and culture are synonymous, it is more appropriate and equitable to design activities based on the histories—the historical *events*, *activities*, and *tools*—of students. Now that we understand this myth, let's explore the cultural values that inspire my work with culturally meaningful practices.

Cultural Values

During my first year of graduate school, an African American professor gave me a binder full of articles on culturally responsive teaching. The professor attended Howard University, where he studied with a prominent scholar in the field. Culturally responsive literature was embedded in his program. I remember reading these articles day and night. For the first time as a student, I read scholarship I could relate to—scholarship that made me reflect on my cultural history. The literature reminded me of my own cultural values and lived experiences. I was intrigued!

My fascination with cultural values inspired me to conduct a master's-level thesis study on them. The title was, *The Effect of Cultural Characteristics in School on Academic Engagement.* Now that I know these cultural values, when students share narratives about their lives and describe community practices, I can place their experiences into buckets based on the eight cultural values I will share with you. You could create other buckets or descriptors of values if you need to. The reason I place them into buckets is to describe the characteristics to others like you. If there were no buckets or names for me to represent these values or interests, it would be challenging to share my experiences with you and describe the values my students embraced. Therefore, rather than using cultural values to predict which students might prefer certain activities in the classroom, I use the values to describe the things students value based on their histories—based on their lived experiences.

African American Psychology

Much of the scholarship I will share in this chapter comes from African American psychology scholarship. Black scholars were inspired to write about the experiences of Black people considering their experiences were excluded in educational and psychological literature or deemed deficient by White scholars, institutions, and science. African American psychology explores African Americans' lived experiences, beliefs, community practices, and cultural values based on group members' descriptions of reality. This contrasts with describing the African American experience from a Eurocentric lens. Much of the early scholarship on Black Psychology emerged in response to educational and psychological theories that described Black people as backward and deficient when compared with White people and mainstream culture (White & Parham, 1990).

Black psychology emerged in response to Western psychology and provides a worldview articulated by Black people themselves rather than relying on concepts and constructs that originated from the minds of White scholars and Western psychology (Belgrave & Allison, 2014; White & Parham, 1990). Like any scientific study, scholars differ in their perspectives, theories, and understanding of African American psychology. However, the theme among all scholars within the field is the need to explore the lived experiences, cultural values, and community practices of Black people by Black people. This contrasts with theories postulated by racist White scholars who contended that Black people were deficient and backward.

Although scholars contend that African American psychology dates to 3200 BC, in ancient Kemet (Egypt) (Belgrave & Allison, 2014; Jamison, 2014; Parham & White, 1990; Parham et al., 2015), I draw from the literature that scholars published dating from the 1960s to now. I have used concepts from this timespan to co-design activities with students and to train educators on culturally meaningful practices. I will share *three* cultural values that scholars associate with traditional Eurocentric, mainstream values, and *five* characteristics scholars associate with traditional African American values.

Consistent with myths related to race and culture, however, I cannot overstate that I do not support the practice of automatically assigning or ascribing values to students based on their race. I cringe at writing "African American values," as I do not believe group members embrace values based solely on their race or ethnicity. Again, it is more accurate to learn about the histories of people and understand events, activities, and tools that shaped their worldviews. However, knowledge related to cultural values and themes helps us describe students' lived experiences and values based on their histories and cultural needs.

I will begin this discussion with three mainstream cultural values that scholars have written extensively about, including *individualism, competition,* and *bureaucratic orientation.* After introducing these concepts, I will describe five cultural values that scholars associate with African American culture, including *communalism, movement expressiveness, orality, verve,* and *affect.* As I share this information, remember that these cultural themes are helpful when we use them to *describe* cultural values and expressions of behaviors; we should not use them to predict student values based on race. As you take notes on these values, remember the words from Boykin and Noguera (2011) that we cannot tell the cultural book by the racial cover.

Individualism

Individualism refers to one's preference for autonomy, independence, individual recognition, solitude, and the exclusion of others (Boykin et al., 2005, p. 532). In the classroom, students who value individualism may prefer to work in isolation from the group; they may engage at a higher level when working autonomously on assignments and disengage when working within groups. Classrooms that promote individualism require students to work in isolation from their peers. Teachers may recognize and praise individual students for accomplishments in these classrooms instead of praising the overall group's efforts.

Competition

Competition refers to one's desire to outperform others in goal-oriented tasks. Individuals who value competition may embrace the idea that, for them to succeed, others must fail, even if "others" include family members and friends. From this perspective, individuals who value competition may perceive friends and family members as competitors and rivals, believing that, to become successful, they must outperform others. Classrooms that promote competition pit students as rivals and encourage them to dominate their peers to succeed. Teachers promote classroom competition by creating activities requiring students to outperform or beat their peers to achieve goals.

Bureaucratic Orientation

Bureaucratic orientation refers to the preference for strict adherence to rules and regulations and reliance on strict punishment policies for individuals who break established rules. Examples of such rules might include:

- don't walk without being told;
- don't speak without raising your hand;
- don't move around in your seat;
- don't tap on your desks; and
- don't speak when the teacher is talking.

Individuals who deviate from these rules and expectations receive consequences throughout the school day and often miss an enormous amount of instructional time due to being removed from the classroom as a punishment for breaking the rules (Williams, 2015). Scholars associate individualism, competition, and bureaucratic orientation with mainstream, Eurocentric values; they argue these themes clash with cultural values many culturally diverse learners embrace.

In my practice as a school psychologist and interventionist, I have worked with students across races and gender who have embraced the abovementioned values. I have also worked with students who resented them. When I coach educators on these cultural values/themes, I encourage them to become aware of them so they can describe preferences in the classroom. This contrasts with using cultural values as guidelines to create activities based on racial and ethnic background. In what follows, I share five cultural themes that clash with the mainstream cultural values mentioned above.

Communalism

Communalism is characterized by four constructs: (1) social orientation; (2) group duty; (3) collective identity; and (4) membership sharing. *Social orientation* refers to preference for social bonds and interconnectedness with people over objects. *Group duty* refers to the belief that one's duty to the group supersedes individualistic duties. *Collective identity* refers to perceiving oneself as part of a collective, and group membership is valued over individualism and materialism. *Membership sharing* is the summation of communalistic constructs in which group members share with one another to accomplish goals, achieve success, and experience psychological and emotional wellness (Boykin et al., 2005).

Scholars contend that individuals who embrace communalism may offer help and resources to others without expecting to receive something in return. Those who embrace communalism may give to others or the group, even if their giving temporarily sets them back. From this perspective, individuals feel a sense of duty to their group and may pride themselves in ensuring that the group succeeds rather than focusing solely on their own success.

Movement Expressiveness

Movement expressiveness comprises at least three values: (1) rhythmic orientation, which is observed in dance movements, preference for percussive music, and daily activities that incorporate stylistic patterns, including speech patterns rhythmically vocalized; (2) a premium placed on rhythmic music that elicits movement, which is needed for ones' psychological well-being; and (3) gestures such as coordinated movements (Allen & Boykin, 1992; Boykin et al., 2005). Individuals who embrace movement expressiveness may have a rhythmic orientation toward life that manifests in (1) their interactions with others; (2) how they convey language; and (3) how they engage with the world.

I have worked with many students who valued music expressiveness and interacted in rhythmic ways in the classroom: they sang songs, danced to beats they created in their heads, rapped lyrics, and tapped their pencils on the desk in rhythmic ways. They engaged in these behaviors during instructional time. They identified instructional activities that included movement expressive themes as engaging and "liked" their teachers who provided this instruction in the classroom. These individuals disengaged when instruction did not include movement expressive activities. Repeatedly, they skipped or got kicked out of class for perceived misbehavior or disrespect.

Orality

Orality represents the vibrancy with which group members express words. Such vibrancy is attached to meaning and sensation. It depends on a "call-and-response" communication (a transactional and continuous dialogue between two or more persons, such that people may be perceived as bored or uninterested if they remain quiet while waiting for their turn to speak) (Boykin et al., 2005).

Speaking is a lively performance not restricted to simply conveying a message (Boykin et al., 2005). Orality was a method of sharing messages and telling and retelling stories within African tribes (Belgrave & Allison, 2014). African

Americans have expressed themselves through rap, storytelling, spoken word, preaching, and teaching, all conveyed through orality (Belgrave & Allison, 2014).

I often share a story about a school district hiring me to work with their staff. While coaching them, they shared that one of their students, an African American third-grade female student, often blurted out responses during instructional time; because she responded rapidly to her teacher's prompts, she never allowed her peers to share their thoughts. The other major issue was that the third grader never raised her hand when she answered. Sometimes the young girl did not give her teacher enough time to finish asking a question. Instead, the girl often responded mid-sentence of the question.

The team created and implemented a behavioral intervention plan (BIP) to stop her "blurt-out behaviors." The intervention effectively stopped her blurt-out behaviors, but in the process, it reduced the student's engagement in general. She stopped responding. In response to her disengagement, the team requested to create a BIP to boost her engagement. The problem was not the student. The problem was that the teacher and student experienced cultural clashes. The teacher had rules and expectations that one student should talk at a time and that students should raise their hands before speaking; those who did not adhere to these rules were punished or recommended for remediation because of their "deficit-based" behaviors.

But the student valued orality. She demonstrated call-response behaviors during instructional time. She often answered her teachers' questions mid-sentence. She also valued communalism in that she aimed to establish relationships with her peers and teacher through her culture. This young Black girl was gifted. She was brilliant. Her memory and recall of information were captivating. She engaged in culturally meaningful ways for her, but her culturally meaningful behaviors clashed with the cultural norms and expectations of the classroom. Not only did the student disengage, but she disliked her teacher because of the constant redirection, correction, and discipline. This cultural clash produced tension between the young girl and her teacher. The girl refused to engage in the classroom and underachieved in the process.

Verve

Verve represents the preference for variability, which stems from expressiveness, bonding, music, movement, and percussiveness. Verve is characterized by three components: (1) lively and intensified behavior; (2) preference for variety and alternations within a setting; and (3) preference for multiple background elements existing simultaneously in one's environment, including activities and stimulation (Boykin et al., 2015). In addition, verve is characterized by rhythm and energy; it may appear in a person's walk, talk, and expressions (Belgrave & Allison, 2014; Williams, 2015).

Affect

The fifth value is affect. I describe affect as being synonymous with emotional engagement. It is engaging with the world emotionally. Boykin et al., 2005 describe it this way:

> The affect cultural theme relates to emotional expressiveness and responsiveness, emphasizing not withholding emotions. Affect attaches meaning to emotional expression (i.e., tone, quality, emphasis, volume, and connotation), as feelings are believed to connect thoughts and behaviors.

I have worked with students who embraced the cultural value affect. When working with them in the classroom, they often expressed themselves by clapping their hands loudly in excitement, dapping their neighbors, and getting out of their seats to dance to celebrate answering a question correctly. They also touched others in the classroom and hugged peers and teachers during instructional time. Teachers often reprimanded students who demonstrated these behaviors in school. Students' cultural values clashed with classroom rules, norms, and expectations. In my experiences as a school psychologist, I have worked with students across races who embraced communalism, movement expressiveness, orality, verve, and affect.

When I coach teachers on cultural values and community practices, I share narratives of how students experienced cultural clashes in the classroom; their cultural values, interests, and literacies collided with classroom rules, norms, and expectations. Students of color often perceived their teachers as racist; teachers perceived their students as unruly, aggressive, oppositional, and violent. When observing these interactions in the classroom, students and teachers were oblivious to the role of culture in teaching and learning. They were unaware of culture's impact on student-teacher relationships and academic engagement. Neither students nor teachers were trained in recognizing cultural clashes in the classroom.

Students and their teachers had cultural needs; students engaged in culturally meaningful ways, and teachers created rules based on their own cultural values. Cultural differences created tension in the classroom. Because teachers and students were unaware of cultural clashes, no one in the classroom could accurately address the problem. Rather than resolving them, cultural clashes persisted throughout the school year. They hurt students in tremendous ways.

For example, students refused to connect with White teachers, social workers, counselors, and deans in the building and disengaged in the classroom. Although they were present in the classroom, in their minds, they "quit school." Teachers referred students for special education services, thinking students' poor response to instruction and intervention stemmed from learning disabilities and emotional challenges that adversely impacted learning. To be sure, students did not have disabilities and teachers were not racist. They experienced cultural clashes that shattered relationships, prevented engagement, and presented as racial tension.

Summary

In this chapter, I shared three cultural values scholars have historically associated with mainstream culture, and five cultural values scholars have associated with traditional African American culture. I discussed the importance of debunking the myth that race and culture are synonymous. I argued that it is most important to use cultural values as descriptors of values rather than to predict which students might embrace specific cultural themes based on their race or ethnicity. I concluded by describing cultural clashes and illustrating how clashes in the classroom often present as racial tension among students of color and White teachers.

What's Next?

In the next chapter, we will unpack the letter *E* of *The LEARN Framework*. Now that we have learned about *The Big Four*–(1) your why; (2) the history of culturally responsive teaching; (3) culturally responsive frameworks; and (4) cultural values and practices–you will have an opportunity in the next chapter to examine your thoughts and feelings about *The Big Four* to prepare for the design process in subsequent chapters.

Chapter 10:

E—Examine

... [Julie] and I belong to a community web ... a Facebook page for the moms in our area, and there was something that was posted [criticizing culturally responsive teaching]. And [Julie] and I, of course, because neither one of us ever keep our mouth shut ... I had to speak up, and we posted—both of us. And you know, we shut them down! Yes, we did. Sit down Karen! Um, so I mean, but it felt good that ... I felt like my, like my response ... I was like, hell yeah! I was like, Yes!—that was, that was good! And [Julie] had a lot to contribute. And not that I couldn't have said something like, you know, last year at this time, based on why something like that [culturally responsive teaching] is beneficial to teachers and students ... but I just felt like I had the research and the history of the theory to say a well thought out statement to someone else who could then be like, oh, okay, maybe I can look into this now and educate myself a little bit better.

—PhD Research Participant

How often do you examine your thoughts, beliefs, and attitudes about education? How often do you interrogate your beliefs and attitudes about culturally meaningful teaching and educational equity?

The letter *E* of *The LEARN Framework* stands for *examine,* and it refers to examining your thoughts, beliefs, and attitudes about culture, culturally responsive education (CRE), and equitable practices.

Research is replete with studies that show the benefits of examining our thoughts, beliefs, and attitudes about educational practices. Geneva Gay, one of the prominent scholars we discussed in Chapter 8, has written extensively about examining and interrogating our thoughts, beliefs, and attitudes to prepare for culturally responsive teaching. Letter *E, examine,* is at the core of culturally meaningful teaching because, in most cases, we practice based on what we believe is true about education. There are decades of research that suggest that we seek to align our practices with our beliefs. For example, if we believe education is the key to success in life, then we will probably seek to motivate our students and children to attain an education.

Similarly, if we believe we should design culturally meaningful practices, we would be more prone to engage in behaviors that would prepare us to develop culturally meaningful activities. If we believe culturally meaningful teaching and equitable practices are irrelevant to education, we will likely avoid books and training sessions on these topics. No matter our position on culturally meaningful teaching and equity, we must examine our thoughts on the subject. We must interrogate our thoughts on why we hold certain beliefs and attitudes about culturally meaningful teaching and equity in the classroom. We will do that in this chapter.

In the previous chapter, I introduced *The Big Four,* which includes learning about—

1. your why;
2. the history of culturally responsive education;
3. culturally responsive frameworks; and
4. cultural values and community practices.

I explained that we must learn about and reflect on *The Big Four* to design culturally meaningful practices with purpose. I argued that if we lack knowledge of culturally meaningful frameworks, it will be impossible to design culturally meaningful practices *intentionally* because culturally meaningful teaching is the application of specific culturally meaningful frameworks.

In this chapter, I create opportunities for you to examine *The Big Four.* By the end of the chapter, you will:

- recognize a special framework to examine your thoughts and feelings, and how thoughts and feelings influence your practices;
- examine your thoughts and feelings related to *The Big Four;*
- examine what your thoughts and feelings make you want to do; and
- examine why culturally meaningful teaching begins in your mind, with thoughts, beliefs, and attitudes related to race, culture, and justice.

I introduce a special framework and activity I use when I coach students and adults through examining and reflecting on their lived experiences. The framework is called *Cognitive-Behavioral Theory,* or CBT for short. This framework is commonly associated with counseling and therapy; counselors and therapists use it as a core tool to help clients become aware of thoughts, feelings, and behaviors, and how thoughts, feelings, and behaviors influence each other.

In what follows, I introduce the *CBT* framework. Then I share activities related to *The Big Four* so you will have an opportunity to examine your thoughts, beliefs, and behaviors as you prepare to design culturally meaningful practices. By the end of the chapter, you will have examined your thoughts, feelings, and behaviors concerning *The Big Four,* which is foundational to culturally meaningful teaching.

Cognitive-Behavioral Theory Framework

Cognitive-behavioral theories suggest our thoughts, feelings, and behaviors influence each other (Famer & Chapman, 2016). From this perspective, our beliefs about people and things affect how we feel and act toward them. As educators, our thoughts influence how we set goals for students in the classroom, interpret students' behaviors, and respond when students experience academic challenges. Figure 5 illustrates the relationship among thoughts, feelings, and behaviors.

Figure 5: Cognitive-Behavioral Theory Triangle

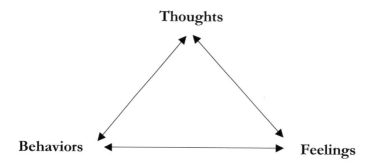

How we think affects how we act and feel

Thoughts

Behaviors   **Feelings**

How we act affects what we think and feel   How we feel affects what we think and do

According to the principles of cognitive-behavioral theory, how we feel about culture, culturally responsive teaching, and equity will influence how we think about these topics, and our thoughts and feelings will influence our behaviors. From this perspective, our practices are rooted in our beliefs, which is why letter *E* of *The LEARN Framework* is at the core of our work with culturally meaningful teaching. I have worked with teachers who claimed to design culturally meaningful practices but described their students and their students' parents, cultures, and communities using deficit-based language.

This happens when we don't examine our thoughts and feelings related to *The Big Four* and examine how our thoughts and feelings make us behave. Observing these experiences has taught me it is possible to hold racist perspectives about students subconsciously while claiming to design culturally meaningful activities for them. In what follows, I include activities related to *The Big Four* so you can examine your thoughts and feelings about these topics.

Activity #1: Examining Your Why

In Chapter 6, I shared the story of Simon Sinek, and I shared that, based on his epiphany, he created a visual that included *what, how,* and *why.* He shared that everyone in business knows what they do; some know how they do it, but very few consider why they do it. I have noticed this perspective applies to culturally responsive teaching. Everyone I have coached has heard of culturally responsive teaching; some knew how to do it; very few were firmly grounded in their why— why they did it or wanted to do it.

Remember, when I mention your *why,* I am referring to your purpose, cause, and core beliefs for why you feel you should or should not design culturally meaningful practices. For example, scholars describe their motivation—their why—for constructing culturally meaningful theories (Ladson-Billings, 1995; Gay, 2014; Paris, 2012). According to CBT, their *thoughts* and *feelings* about racist theories motivated them to produce alternative views to explain underachievement among students of color. Their thoughts and feelings inspired them to articulate the need to pair students' cultural values, community practices, and lived experiences with instruction.

In Chapter 6, you reflected on your why. In Chapter 7, after learning about the history of CRE, you reconsidered your why. For the next activity, I want you to *examine* your why. Using the CBT triangle in Figure 6, reflect on your thoughts about your why. Think about what your why is (thoughts), how your why makes you feel (feelings), and what your thoughts and feelings make you do—or want to do—in practice (behaviors).

Figure 6: Cognitive-Behavioral Theory Triangle

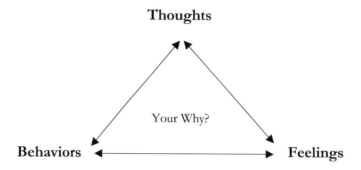

How we think affects how we act and feel

Thoughts

Your Why?

Behaviors   **Feelings**

How we act affects what we think and feel   How we feel affects what we think and do

In the space below, use the four columns to examine how your thoughts, feelings, and behaviors influence each other—and what your next steps will be, considering your beliefs and attitudes about your why. In the *thoughts* column, jot down your why and any thoughts about your why. Then, jot down how those thoughts make you feel in the feelings column. In the *behaviors* column, jot down what your thoughts and feelings make you do in practice or what they make you want to do regarding culturally responsive teaching.

For example, your thoughts and feelings might make you want to share with others what you have learned about culturally responsive teaching or make you want to design culturally responsive activities. In the *Next Step?* column, jot down what you will do next—what you will do moving forward—considering your beliefs and attitudes related to your why. In Table 4, I provide an example of what I am suggesting. I show how my thoughts, feelings, and behaviors influence my purpose for designing and implementing culturally responsive teaching.

Table 4: Example of Thoughts, Feelings, Behaviors Reflection Activity—My Why

Thoughts	Feelings	Behaviors	Next Step?
Students come from rich cultures, and their cultures, community practices, and lived experiences should be a part of classroom instruction. All teachers can become competent at designing culturally responsive practices. I believe all teachers can learn to develop activities related to their subject areas.	I often get frustrated when I think about how some students come to school and never get to learn using their cultural values, lived experiences, and community practices. It's frustrating to know that whenever their racial groups are mentioned, the discussion centers on deficit-based perspectives and negativity. However, it feels good to know that teachers can learn to improve their practices in culturally meaningful ways.	I co-design culturally meaningful activities with students to ensure that their cultural interests and lived experiences are a part of the learning experience. In addition, I have conversations about the need for culturally responsive teaching with stakeholders, and I design and publish training materials such as this book to coach stakeholders through designing culturally meaningful practices.	I will continue to connect with students to learn about their cultural values, community practices, and lived experiences. I will continue to co-design activities with them and place their experiences and values at the center of instruction. I will also create opportunities for them to identify their cultural values and learn how their values may clash with school cultural norms.

In Table 4, I examined the relationship among my thoughts, feelings, and behaviors in practice. As you reflect on my example, notice I started with thoughts, then discussed how my thoughts affect my feelings and how my thoughts and feelings affect my behaviors. When you use the CBT image (Figure 6), remember the bidirectional arrows. These arrows suggest that the framework is not linear. Thoughts, feelings, and behaviors influence each other bidirectionally (as illustrated in Figure 6). Table 5 is workspace for you to examine the relationship among your thoughts, feelings, and behaviors concerning your why. The bidirectional lines suggest that our thoughts, feelings, and behaviors affect us bi-directionally rather than linearly.

Examining Thoughts, Feelings, and Behaviors Related to Your *Why*

Table 5: Thoughts, Feelings, Behaviors Activity

Thoughts ←	Feelings	Behaviors →	Next Step?

Now that you have examined the relationship among your thoughts, feelings, and behaviors related to your why, document how you will achieve your *Next Step* goal and determine what tools you will use to achieve it.

Examining Your Thoughts, Feelings, and Behaviors Related to the History of CRE

As you used the CBT framework and table to examine your thoughts, feelings, and behaviors related to your why, this section provides an opportunity for you to examine your thoughts and feelings related to the history of CRE and how your thoughts and feelings affect your behaviors. In Table 6, I examine my thoughts and feelings about the history of CRE, and I share how my thoughts and feelings affect my behaviors. I then share my *Next Step* goal.

My Example—The History of CRE

Table 6: Example of Thoughts, Feelings, Behaviors Reflection Activity—History of CRE

Thoughts ←	Feelings	Behaviors →	Next Step?
It is astounding to know that scholars wrote and published articles describing students of color and students from impoverished backgrounds as genetically and culturally deficient and incapable of learning because of their race and class. Researchers published this scholarship as recently as the 1960s and 1970s. It is heartbreaking to know that scholars continued to write about similar theories into the 1990s (**NOTE**: I did not discuss this literature in this book). We must debunk deficit-based beliefs so that we do not follow the thinking of racist scholars of the 1960s and 1970s.	I feel disgusted to know that scholars published racist research and scholarship to describe the underperformance of students of color and students from impoverished backgrounds. It frustrates me when I think about how some people still believe we should not teach students about their own cultures in the classroom or pair their cultures, community practices, and lived experiences with instruction.	I share the history of culturally responsive education with stakeholders. I design culturally responsive practices because, unlike racist scholars of the 1960s and 1970s, I do not believe students are genetically or culturally deficient. Instead, I believe they come from rich cultural backgrounds, which is why I center their cultures in the classroom.	I am excited that you and other stakeholders are using this book to design culturally meaningful practices because the tools in this book will guide you and other readers through developing culturally meaningful practices. I will follow up with you and other readers using this book and create additional training resources for you all on designing culturally meaningful practices.

Table 7 is workspace for you to examine the relationship among your thoughts, feelings, and behaviors about the history of CRE.

Examining Thoughts, Feelings, and Behaviors Related to the History of CRE

Table 7: Thoughts, Feelings, Behaviors Activity

Thoughts	Feelings	Behaviors	Next Step?

Now that you have examined the relationship among your thoughts, feelings, and behaviors related to the history of CRE, document how you will achieve your *Next Step* goal and determine what tools you will use to achieve it.

Examining Your Thoughts, Feelings, and Behaviors Related to Culturally Meaningful Frameworks

When I train educators on culturally meaningful teaching, they often share they do not use frameworks. Some educators have told me they did not want any theories; they wanted quick tip solutions—interventions. The problem, which you now know, is that culturally meaningful teaching is applying theories and theoretical frameworks in the classroom. Therefore, to design culturally meaningful practices *intentionally*, you must know and use these frameworks as guides to design culturally meaningful practices.

In this section, we will examine our thoughts, feelings, and behaviors related to the importance of culturally meaningful teaching frameworks, and we will determine our next step, considering our thoughts and attitudes related to frameworks. In Table 8, I examine my thoughts, feelings, and behaviors about culturally meaningful frameworks. I then share how I will respond moving forward.

Table 8: Example of Thoughts, Feelings, Behaviors Reflection Activity—Frameworks

Thoughts	Feelings	Behaviors	Next Step?
Culturally meaningful teaching is applying culturally meaningful principles that make up the framework. Educators struggle with culturally meaningful teaching because they lack knowledge of culturally meaningful frameworks. If they learn about frameworks and how to apply them, they will make tremendous gains in their knowledge about culturally meaningful teaching and designing culturally meaningful practices.	I feel good knowing that I now have a framework for practice so that I can coach educators on how to design culturally meaningful activities (*The LEARN Framework*). It feels good knowing all teachers can learn to develop culturally meaningful practices no matter their race, gender, or culture— and I feel hopeful that stakeholders will design culturally meaningful practices intentionally.	I provide training on culturally meaningful teaching, and I coach educators through applying frameworks in the classroom. I now coach educators through designing culturally meaningful practices using *The LEARN Framework*. I have created online curricula on *The LEARN Framework for Practice* so stakeholders can have step-by-step resources to guide them through the design process. I have also established The *LEARN Academy,* an online academy filled with coaching modules dedicated to using *The LEARN Framework* to design MTSS programming, including instructional support across tiers, transformative SEL activities, and trauma-informed practices.	I will continue providing coaching opportunities for educators who use this book as a guide to design culturally meaningful practices. I will continue to design and publish modules for stakeholders who enroll in *The LEARN Academy.*

Table 9 is workspace for you to examine the relationship among your thoughts, feelings, and behaviors as they relate to culturally meaningful teaching frameworks.

Examining Thoughts, Feelings, and Behaviors Related to Culturally Meaningful Frameworks

Table 9: Thoughts, Feelings, Behaviors Activity

Thoughts	Feelings	Behaviors	Next Step?

Now that you have examined the relationship among your thoughts, feelings, and behaviors related to culturally meaningful frameworks, document how you will achieve your *Next Step* goal and determine what tools you will use to achieve it.

Examining Your Thoughts, Feelings, and Behaviors Related to Cultural Values and Community Practices

Finally, I will create an opportunity for you to examine your thoughts on cultural values and community practices. When I train educators on my work, I often share that, from my experiences attending PD training on culturally meaningful teaching as a school psychologist, I understand how these training sessions go; many trainers spend a lot of time on race, racism, and White privilege, and they ignore the implications of culture and cultural clashes in the classroom.

Cultural clashes explain one reason students disengage at a high level in the classroom. From this perspective, the cultural values of students and teachers clash in the classroom. For example, students may embrace communalism, movement expressiveness, and orality while learning, whereas their teachers may value individualism and competition and create strict rules to govern the classroom. When I provide training for districts that disproportionately refer and qualify students of color for special education services, I show how cultural clashes in the classroom contribute to disproportionality rooted in inequity.

Considering cultural clashes contribute to student disengagement and poor student-teacher relationships, we must be aware of the power of culture and cultural conflicts in the classroom. Therefore, we must examine our cultural values and reflect on how we insert our cultural preferences into the classroom during instructional time. In what follows, I include an activity that will allow you to examine your thoughts, feelings, and behaviors about cultural values.

We will explore which cultural values we embrace in our daily lives and examine the cultural values we embrace in our practice—in classrooms, in counseling groups, and when providing educational support in general. Scholars often present cultural values as dichotomous values, in which they argue that we *either* embrace individualism *or* communalism. I don't see it this way.

From my experiences providing educational support for thousands of students and from coaching hundreds of teachers on culturally meaningful teaching, I have found that we embrace an array of cultural values I described in Chapter 9—i.e., individualism, communalism, bureaucratic orientation, and so on—but we prefer certain values at specific times. The question becomes, when do you prefer *individualism*? When do you prefer *communalism*? When do you prefer *movement expressive activities*? When do you prefer *rhythm, music,* and other cultural elements? I often say we all fall on a cultural continuum. Figure 7 illustrates how the continuum looks when considering individualism and communalism.

Figure 7: The Cultural Continuum

The Cultural Continuum

Individualism   Communalism

$\longleftrightarrow$

Most people I have trained embraced both individualism and communalism. However, they preferred elements of individualism at specific times and with particular activities and aspects of communalism at other times. From this perspective, when considering *The Cultural Continuum*, educators fell on the left, closer to individualism with certain things, and with others, closer to the right. From this perspective, they embraced both values based on specific life situations and events. Awareness of your cultural values—how you insert your values in the classroom when creating rules and providing instruction—and how your values clash with your students' values are at the core of culturally meaningful teaching.

This section includes two sets of activities to help you examine cultural values you embrace. In the first set, I include a table that briefly redefines each cultural value. In the far-left column, I include a list of cultural values; in the middle column,

I define each cultural value; in the far-right column, I include space for you to place an "x" to signify the cultural values you embrace. For this activity, you will determine which cultural values you embrace as an individual. Below the table, you will have an opportunity to describe when you might embrace those values. In Table 10, I provide an example of how you should engage with the activity.

Cultural Values I Embrace in General

Table 10: Example of Cultural Values Activity

Cultural Values	Definitions	X
Individualism	a preference for autonomy, independence, recognition, solitude, and excluding of others	x
Competition	feeling the need to be the best that you can be *and* using your abilities to outperform others	x
Bureaucracy Orientation	reliance on a strict list of rules *and* punishing individuals who do not obey those rules	x
Communalism	preference for interdependence, community, and group sharing	x
Movement Expressiveness	preference for syncopated music, dance, rhythm, percussiveness	x
Orality	preference for using spoken word in creative ways and value of oral expression to convey feelings	x
Verve	preference for stimulation and variability, including engagement in more than one activity at once	x
Affect	value of expressing the self emotionally—not "withholding or restraining emotions"	x

In Table 10, I placed a checkmark next to each cultural value, indicating that I embrace all eight. But here is what I want you to focus on. The question becomes, when do I prefer these cultural values, and how might they increase or decrease the likelihood I might engage or disengage in some activity? I will briefly share a story to illustrate my value for individualism and communalism and how these values influence how I select which activities to participate in.

While writing my dissertation, one of my advisors created opportunities for students to write as a collective on certain days and times throughout the week. He did this by sending out Zoom links where students could access the writing location during those days and times to write as a collective on dissertation content. I am unsure how many students signed up for this opportunity, but I did not participate. Although I thought this was a fantastic opportunity for students who enjoyed writing as a collective, I would not have enjoyed it, and here is why.

When I write, I like being alone and playing music. I'll describe my writing experience as a "vibing process" in which I become one with the background music, the material I am reading, and the thoughts generated from the reading material. My response to what I read and reflect on—my writing—consists of these elements. I enjoy creative writing and writing alone, mainly when working on something significant. I don't like being distracted by others—I am easily distracted—and I don't like being interrupted when I'm writing. I like to flow with my background elements, reading materials, and insights I generate in response to this learning environment.

If I had to write with others, I might not engage at a high level, and I do not think I could produce the quality of ideas I might create if I worked in isolation from others. As a creative writer, I prefer a particular learning environment where I am alone, listening to music, and writing. However, this does not mean I do not value communalism and working as a collective. For example, based on the following facts about me, would you say I value communalism?

- I often place the group over myself.
- I value working interdependently on designing lessons and problem solving.

- I value helping others when they are in need without the expectation of receiving something in return.
- I value giving to others, even if my giving sets me back temporarily.
- My sense of self is within the context of the group, as in the African proverb—*I am because we are, and we are because I am.*

Would you regard these values as elements of individualism or communalism? Communalism, right? I prefer the group, group belonging, working interdependently, and so on—all elements of communalism. Therefore, I value both individualism and communalism. Therefore, instead of asking if I prefer individualism *or* communalism, better questions are: When might I prefer elements of individualism and communalism? When might I prefer activities that incorporate elements of individualism, and when might I prefer activities that incorporate elements of communalism? Essentially, we all fall on the cultural continuum I described above. We might fall to the far left, near individualism, and at other times, we may fall to the far right, near communalism. In what follows, I present the first activity, giving you an opportunity to identify cultural values you embrace among the eight.

Activity 1—Cultural Values You Embrace

In Table 11, place an x in the X column next to the cultural values you embrace as an individual. Then, after you mark the cultural themes you value, use the workspace below to examine your interests concerning those values and when you might prefer them.

Table 11: Cultural Values Activity

Cultural Values	Definitions	X
Individualism	a preference for autonomy, independence, recognition, solitude, and excluding of others	
Competition	feeling the need to be the best that you can be *and* using your abilities to outperform others	
Bureaucracy Orientation	reliance on a strict list of rules *and* punishing individuals who do not obey those rules	
Communalism	preference for interdependence, community, and group sharing	
Movement Expressiveness	preference for syncopated music, dance, rhythm, percussiveness	
Orality	preference for using spoken word in creative ways and value of oral expression to convey feelings	
Verve	preference for stimulation and variability, including engagement in more than one activity at once	
Affect	value of expressing the self emotionally—not "withholding or restraining emotions"	

Now that you have placed a checkmark next to the cultural values you embrace In Table 11, use the workspace below to examine your interests concerning those values and when you might prefer activities that highlight the values. Refer to my story above with individualism and communalism to help you determine when you might prefer different values.

Guiding questions are:

- When do I prefer activities that emphasize individualism?
- When do I prefer activities that emphasize communalism?
- When do I prefer movement expressive activities?
- Which elements of orality do I value?
- When do I engage in behaviors that reflect orality?
- When do I prefer competition?
- When do I value creating strict rules and punishing others when they do not obey them?

Share your thoughts about the values you selected in Table 11. Write about when you might prefer activities related to each value.

Activity #1b: Examining Preference for Cultural Values in Your Life

For the second set of activities, you will determine which cultural values influence your instructional practices, and you'll have an opportunity to examine your practices to determine how those values play out in your classroom. In Table 12, I provide an example of how you should engage with the activity. I identify which cultural values influence my instructional practices.

Examining Which Cultural Values Influence My Instructional Practices

Table 12: Examining Cultural Values and Instructional Practices Activity Example

Cultural Values	Definitions	X
Individualism	a preference for autonomy, independence, recognition, solitude, and excluding of others	
Competition	feeling the need to be the best that you can be *and* using your abilities to outperform others	
Bureaucracy Orientation	reliance on a strict list of rules *and* punishing individuals who do not obey those rules	
Communalism	preference for interdependence, community, and group sharing	x
Movement Expressiveness	preference for syncopated music, dance, rhythm, percussiveness	x
Orality	preference for using spoken word in creative ways and value of oral expression to convey feelings	x
Verve	preference for stimulation and variability, including engagement in more than one activity at once	x
Affect	value of expressing the self emotionally—not "withholding or restraining emotions"	x

Cultural themes that dominate my practices in the classroom include communalism, movement expressiveness, orality, verve, and affect. In these spaces, my main goal is to build a "family-like" community. I co-design activities with and for students based on their cultural interests. Often, activities incorporate hip-hop, rhythm and blues (R&B), and Reggaeton music; students express themselves, process information, and demonstrate mastery of learning through the arts, including rapping, singing, dancing, and drawing.

All five cultural values I checked in Table 12 influence my practices. I did not check bureaucracy orientation as a cultural theme because students and I do not establish a long list of strict rules in these learning spaces, and even if students break the limited rules we establish, I rarely ever punish them (as in intentionally giving them a punitive consequence); instead, we talk about and learn from the experience.

Because of the high level of engagement during instructional time, students formed authentic and lasting relationships with their teachers whom I co-led lessons with; they also bonded with each other in the classroom. Since I am aware of the cultural themes I incorporate in the classroom, I can reflect on my experiences as an educator and determine if my cultural values clash with my students' values. I can do this because I have knowledge of cultural values, and I regularly examine my practices to determine if my cultural ways of being clash with the ways my students prefer to learn. Knowing cultural values is why I can differentiate instructional practices by culture. If students do not embrace cultural values or specific activities, I problem-solve with them to adjust instructional activities to meet their needs. Next, I present the second set of activities, giving you an opportunity to explore cultural values that influence your instructional practices.

Activity 2: Examining Which Cultural Values Influence Your Instructional Practices

Place an "x" in the far-right column to indicate which cultural values influence your instructional practices:

Table 13: Cultural Values and Instructional Practices

Cultural Values	Definitions	X
Individualism	a preference for autonomy, independence, recognition, solitude, and excluding of others	
Competition	feeling the need to be the best that you can be *and* using your abilities to outperform others	
Bureaucracy Orientation	reliance on a strict list of rules *and* punishing individuals who do not obey those rules	
Communalism	preference for interdependence, community, and group sharing	
Movement Expressiveness	preference for syncopated music, dance, rhythm, percussiveness	
Orality	preference for using spoken word in creative ways and value of oral expression to convey feelings	
Verve	preference for stimulation and variability, including engagement in more than one activity at once	
Affect	value of expressing the self emotionally—not "withholding or restraining emotions"	

Now that you have selected the values that influence your instructional practices, use the workspace below to examine how you insert those values in the classroom. Use these guiding questions as prompts:

- How do the cultural values you placed a checkmark next to influence how you create rules during instructional time?
- How do the cultural values you placed a checkmark next to influence your instructional practices (i.e., designing your lessons, ways of providing instruction, behavioral expectations for your lessons, and so on)?

- How might the cultural values you placed a checkmark next to clash with the cultural values of your students in general and students of color in particular?

Document your thoughts to these questions in the workspace below.

Activity 2b: Examining How Cultural Values Influence Your Practices

Now that you've documented how cultural values influence your instructional practices, let's be a bit more explicit about how the cultural values influence your practices. Just for a moment, think about the many activities you share in the classroom during instructional time. Now, in the left column of Table 14, jot down instructional activities you implement in your classroom. In the right column, determine which cultural value(s) the activity might align with. I include the eight cultural values below for this activity, and I provide examples for you in the columns in Table 14 to illustrate how to engage with the activity.

Cultural Values:

1. Individualism
2. Competition
3. Bureaucracy Orientation
4. Communalism
5. Movement Expressiveness
6. Orality
7. Verve
8. Affection

Table 14: Examining Instructional Practices and Cultural Values

Document your instructional practices and cultural values associated with those practices.

Activity 2C: Examining Instructional Practices and Cultural Values

Instructional Practices	Cultural Values
i.e., Cooperative Learning Activities	i.e., Communalism and Orality

Table 14 allows you to put your practices on paper and consider which cultural values influence them. From this activity, you can consider a list of questions concerning your practices and cultural values, including:

- Which cultural values aligns with instructional activities you listed in the table?
- Which cultural values *dominate* your instructional practices?
- Who benefits from the activities and cultural values?
- Who disengages because of the activities and cultural values?
- Which cultural values are excluded from instructional activities?

Prior to reading this book, when was the last time you reflected on cultural values and how they influence your practices as an educator? When was the last time you reflected on how your activities and cultural values associated with those activities might contribute to student disengagement and poor student-teacher relationship? The goal of the activities in this chapter was to create an opportunity for you to examine cultural values and how teaching and learning is a sociocultural process.

I encourage you to continue reading about cultural values and examine how they are present in your practices. I also recommend you continue reading about community practices and activities students engage with within their homes and communities. While there are many community practices you can draw from, I often incorporate the arts with instruction because students request them. If you are interested in learning more about community practices and how to pair them with instruction, join *The Redesign* private Facebook group, where I include additional resources, including coaching videos on the topics in this book.

If you want step-by-step coaching, enroll in *The LEARN Academy,* where I will coach you and provide a deep dive into the design process related to my work with *The LEARN Framework* and designing culturally meaningful practices. I am so confident that you will learn to design culturally meaningful activities in *The LEARN Academy*, using my coaching and design principles, that I offer a money-back guarantee option!

Summary

In this chapter, I introduced the letter *E* of *The LEARN Framework*, which stands for *examine*, and I discussed the importance of examining your thoughts about culturally responsive teaching. I included two sets of activities for you to examine the relationship among your thoughts, feelings, and behaviors, as they pertain to culturally meaningful teaching.

What's Next?

In the next chapter, I will revisit culturally meaningful frameworks and show you exactly how to apply them so you can design culturally meaningful practices. I will guide you through a simple strategy you can use to develop culturally meaningful activities—the same strategy I taught practitioners in my study. Get ready to start designing culturally meaningful practices with confidence!

Chapter 11:

A—Adopt/Apply a Culturally Meaningful Framework

It was really helpful to have the table [Culturally Meaningful Comparison Table] that included the prominent scholar, definition, guiding principles, and prominent article. I was able to use that to guide me in everything that I did. The only problem is that I still need the table.

—PhD Research Participant

When was the last training you received on culturally responsive teaching that addressed the importance of applying culturally responsive frameworks when designing culturally responsive activities? The letter *A* of *The LEARN Framework for Practice* stands for adopt/apply and means adopting and applying a culturally meaningful framework when developing culturally meaningful practices.

Becoming competent at culturally responsive teaching requires that you learn about culturally meaningful frameworks and how to apply them to design culturally meaningful practices. One reason practitioners struggled to develop culturally responsive activities before participating in my research study was that they had never been trained on culturally responsive frameworks. All practitioners explained that they had never received training on culturally responsive frameworks and did not discuss culturally responsive teaching during their teacher training programs. They had never read a book about culturally responsive frameworks or attended PD training on the topic. Instead, their training on culturally responsive teaching included discussions on race, White privilege, rigorous instruction, and technical quick-tip solutions.

Because of their lack of knowledge—among other barriers—practitioners started the study not knowing how to design culturally meaningful practices. Some doubted their ability to create activities because of these challenges. By the end of the training, however, all practitioners used frameworks to design culturally meaningful practices. They identified frameworks as the most helpful resource for helping them design culturally meaningful practices.

In this chapter, I re-introduce the frameworks discussed during *The Big Four* and show how practitioners and I used them to design culturally meaningful practices. By the end of this chapter, you will understand:

- the significance of applying culturally meaningful frameworks when designing culturally meaningful activities;
- how to apply culturally responsive principles when designing culturally meaningful practices; and
- how to convert culturally meaningful framework principles into goals and objectives when planning for any lesson.

Throughout this chapter, I provide practical tips on how to use culturally meaningful frameworks in the classroom; a key feature is providing guidance on creating learning objectives using culturally meaningful principles. Finally, I conclude the chapter by sharing a vignette that illustrates the benefits of using frameworks to design culturally meaningful activities.

I begin this discussion by introducing what I call, *The Culturally Meaningful Comparison Table* (see Table 15). I call it this because it includes three prominent frameworks, and while all three have things in common, each framework has a special meaning based on principles. When we use the frameworks, we create culturally meaningful—i.e., culturally *relevant*, culturally *responsive*, or culturally *sustaining*—activities.

In my study, practitioners used these tables to design culturally meaningful activities. Specifically, two educators designed culturally *relevant* activities according to Ladson-Billings' (1995) framework, and five practitioners designed culturally *responsive* activities based on Gay's (2014) framework. In addition, two practitioners (of the seven) used principles from multiple frameworks, in eclectic ways. In what follows, I show you exactly how to use *The Culturally Meaningful Comparison Table* to design culturally meaningful practices.

Table 15: Culturally Meaningful Comparison Table

Frameworks:	Culturally *Relevant* Pedagogy	Culturally *Responsive* Teaching	Culturally *Sustaining* Pedagogy
Scholar:	Gloria Ladson-Billings	Geneva Gay	Django Paris
Definitions:	"A pedagogy of opposition, not unlike critical pedagogy, but specifically committed to collective, not merely individual empowerment" (Ladson-Billings, 1995, p. 160).	"Culturally responsive teaching uses the cultural orientations, heritages, and background experiences of students of color as referents and resources to improve their school achievement" (Gay, 2014, p. 357).	A pedagogy that "seeks to perpetuate and foster—to sustain—linguistic, literate, and cultural pluralism as part of the democratic project of schooling" (Paris, 2012, p. 93).
Guiding Principles:	1. Students will experience academic success. 2. Students will develop/maintain cultural competence and academic excellence. 3. Students will develop a critical consciousness through which they challenge the status quo and current social order (Ladson-Billings, 1995. pp. 160-161).	1. A need to teach to and through students. 2. A need to build bridges for teachers and students to cross. 3. Race, ethnicity, and culture matter profoundly in teaching and learning. 4. Changing perceptions of underachieving students from problems to possibilities (Gay, 2014, pp. 357-359).	1. A focus on the plural and evolving nature of **youth identity** and **cultural practices** and a commitment to embracing youth culture's counter-hegemonic potential; 2. While maintaining a clear-eyed critique of how youth culture can also reproduce systemic inequalities (Paris & Alim, 2014, p. 85).
Prominent Article:	Ladson-Billings, G. (1995). But that's just good teaching! The case for culturally relevant pedagogy.	Gay, G. (2014). Preparing for culturally responsive teaching.	Paris, D. (2012). Culturally sustaining pedagogy: A needed change in stance, terminology, and practice.

All practitioners in my study commented that this table was the most helpful resource for helping them understand culturally responsive teaching and designing culturally responsive practices. I will briefly discuss the comparison table, then describe how I guided practitioners through using this table during the research study to unpack culturally meaningful teaching and design culturally meaningful activities.

Before the study, I searched for a resource that compared the three frameworks side-by-side, as illustrated in the comparison table above. I felt I could use this to compare culturally responsive frameworks, their definitions, and their guiding principles to show how frameworks were similar and different from each other. I wanted to show that culturally responsive teaching has a variety of definitions and that there are similar and different guiding principles within each framework. However, I could not find a table that was this specific, so I compiled resources and designed the table myself. I believed teachers needed to understand:

- culturally responsive frameworks;
- prominent scholars who currently write about culturally responsive education;
- definitions of culturally responsive teaching; and
- guiding principles that comprise culturally responsive frameworks.

My main goal in designing this table was to reveal that there are multiple frameworks of culturally responsive teaching, numerous scholars who write about culturally responsive teaching, and multiple definitions of culturally responsive teaching. I also wanted to illustrate that each framework comprises "guiding principles" that practitioners can use as guides to design culturally responsive practices. From this perspective, when we say we are designing culturally responsive activities, we are saying we are following one of the scholar's frameworks above or some other culturally meaningful framework to guide our practices.

The *Culturally Meaningful Comparison Table* is a part of *The LEARN Framework* we have been unpacking since Chapter 3. My goal in writing this book was to share with you *The LEARN Framework for Practice* so you can use it to unpack culturally responsive teaching and design culturally responsive practices. Now that I have addressed the letters *L* (learn) and *E* (examine), I will describe how we applied the framework in my research study. I will teach you how you can use it in your practice to design culturally meaningful activities. I will not spend much time discussing the details of the table or each framework. Still, I will provide the steps we took that led to learning about culturally meaningful teaching and using frameworks to design culturally meaningful practices. Finally, I will share what we did during the research study from meetings 1 through 7.

Applying Frameworks in Practice

My guess is that you don't sit around and reflect on frameworks, but an array of frameworks and principles guide your practices. You probably learned these principles and frameworks during your teacher training program, and when you taught, you applied them in the classroom. For example, many teachers use *scaffolding* techniques, incorporate *positive* and *negative reinforcement* strategies, and provide *social and emotional learning* (SEL) support.

Scaffolding techniques are associated with Russian psychologist Lev Vygotsky's learning principles. Positive and negative reinforcement are associated with behavioral psychology principles related to manipulating behavior, and SEL is associated with various psychological and educational principles related to social and emotional learning. Therefore, scaffolding in the classroom is the *application* of Lev Vygotsky's work; providing positive and negative reinforcement is the *application* of behavioral psychology principles; and implementing SEL supports is the *application* of a host of educational and psychological principles related to social and emotional learning.

My point in sharing this information about theories, principles, and frameworks is that teaching in the classroom is *applying* a host of concepts and principles related to some framework. Culturally responsive teaching is no different; it *applies* principles related to culturally responsive education (CRE). A major reason practitioners struggle to design culturally meaningful practices is that they are unfamiliar with culturally meaningful frameworks. From this perspective, they cannot use culturally meaningful frameworks as guides to design culturally meaningful activities. In what follows, I will revisit the three culturally meaningful frameworks that are a part of *The Big Four*, and I will share how practitioners applied them in the study to design culturally meaningful SEL activities.

Applying Culturally Responsive Teaching Frameworks

After engaging practitioners in activities related to *The Big Four*, I reintroduced Ladson-Billings' (1995), Gay's (2014), and Paris's (2012) frameworks. My goal was to coach educators through applying frameworks to design culturally meaningful practices. Here is how I did it. I—

1. reintroduced each framework and discussed principles that compose the frameworks;
2. encouraged practitioners to select one of the three frameworks to guide their designs;
3. urged practitioners to use the principles of the framework to design culturally meaningful SEL practices; and
4. encouraged them to describe how their designs were culturally meaningful by explaining how they used principles to guide their designs.

Practitioners and I worked collectively through this process. I thought it was essential to do this as a collective so I could understand the problems practitioners experienced with applying frameworks. After I provided examples on how to design based on all three frameworks, and after practitioners shared examples to demonstrate their understanding, I gave them all design templates. Their homework was designing culturally meaningful SEL activities and presenting them in the following session. All practitioners were well familiar with SEL, as their district had been implementing SEL programming in the classroom for over ten years at the time of the study.

Initially, I planned to include examples of design templates in this book, but I had reservations: I felt it would be more effective to present the design templates *and* show you how to use them. Therefore, instead of simply including blank design templates at the end of this book, I have included them in our private Facebook group: *Redesign: An SEL Toolkit for Designing Culturally Meaningful Practices.* In this group, I have created how-to videos to show you exactly how to use the design templates to critique and problematize your lessons (which is the first step in redesigning your practices). After problematizing your current practices, I will show you how to use the templates to redesign your practices in culturally meaningful ways. Be sure to join us in the private group if you are interested in learning how to use design templates to develop culturally meaningful activities.

In what follows, I will guide you through the exact process I showed practitioners in my study so you can understand how to apply culturally meaningful frameworks to design culturally meaningful activities.

1. Reintroduce Culturally Responsive Frameworks

As I did with teachers and administrators in my study, I will reintroduce the three frameworks we discussed during the *L* component of *The LEARN Framework.* Each framework is included in Table 16.

Table 16: Reintroducing Culturally Meaningful Comparison Table

Frameworks:	Culturally *Relevant*	Culturally *Responsive*	Culturally *Sustaining*
Scholar:	Gloria Ladson-Billings	Geneva Gay	Django Paris
Definitions:	"A pedagogy of opposition, not unlike critical pedagogy, but specifically committed to collective, not merely individual empowerment" (Ladson-Billings, 1995, p. 160).	"Culturally responsive teaching uses the cultural orientations, heritages, and background experiences of students of color as referents and resources to improve their school achievement" (Gay, 2014, p. 357).	A pedagogy that "seeks to perpetuate and foster—to sustain—linguistic, literate, and cultural pluralism as part of the democratic project of schooling" (Paris, 2012, p. 93).
Guiding Principles:	1. Students will experience academic success. 2. Students will develop/maintain cultural competence and academic excellence. 3. Students will develop a critical consciousness through which they challenge the status quo and current social order (Ladson-Billings, 1995, pp. 160-161).	1. A need to teach to and through students. 2. A need to build bridges for teachers and students to cross. 3. Race, ethnicity, and culture matter profoundly in teaching and learning. 4. Changing perceptions of underachieving students from problems to possibilities (Gay, 2014, pp. 357-359).	1. A focus on the plural and evolving nature of **youth identity** and **cultural practices** and a commitment to embracing youth culture's counter-hegemonic potential; 2. While maintaining a clear-eyed critique of how youth culture can also reproduce systemic inequalities (Paris & Alim, 2014, p. 85).
Prominent Article:	Ladson-Billings, G. (1995). But that's just good teaching! The case for culturally relevant pedagogy.	Gay, G. (2014). Preparing for culturally responsive teaching.	Paris, D. (2012). Culturally sustaining pedagogy: A needed change in stance, terminology, and practice.

2. Select One of the Three Frameworks to Guide Your Design

You learned about culturally responsive teaching frameworks during the letter *L* component (learn) of *The LEARN Framework.* You examined your thoughts and attitudes related to these frameworks during letter *E* (examine*)*. When I introduced the letter *L* of the framework, I explained that it was vital for you to learn about *The Big Four,* which was the goal of the letter *L.* I recommended that you take detailed notes on *The Big Four.* It was vital that you dedicated sufficient time to learn letter *L* content because you will now apply that knowledge as you design culturally meaningful activities.

Letter *A* of *The LEARN Framework* is about adopting and applying a framework to design culturally meaningful activities. Now that you know culturally responsive frameworks, you will select a framework to guide you as you design culturally meaningful practices. You will choose from the three choices I listed in the table above, the same frameworks I introduced during *The Big Four*—either Ladson-Billings' (1995), Gay's (2014), or Paris's (2012) framework (see the "culturally relevant," "culturally responsive," and "culturally sustaining" columns in Table 16).

3. Use the Principles of Your Framework to Design Activities

Designing culturally responsive practices is applying culturally meaningful principles. A highly effective method of applying principles when designing instruction is turning them into goals and objectives. Practitioners in my research study found this approach effective in guiding them through designing culturally meaningful activities. To apply this method, you will have to know the difference between overall *goals* and specific, measurable *objectives.*

For this activity, I define educational goals as broad, overall objectives we seek to achieve when designing a lesson; we achieve goals by creating specific, measurable objectives related to the goal. Here is how the strategy works: Turn each culturally responsive principle into a goal, then create specific measurable objectives within your lesson to achieve the goal. Practitioners in my research study found this strategy effective at re-imagining their practices in culturally meaningful ways. Next, I will show you how to apply this strategy.

Notice the "guiding principles" row in Tables 15 and 16. I included three guiding principles from Ladson-Billings' culturally *relevant* framework, four guiding principles from Gay's culturally *responsive* framework, and two principles from Paris's culturally *sustaining* framework. Now here is the trick that will help you apply the frameworks—make the principles broad, overall goals. Let's use Ladson-Billings' (1995) culturally relevant framework, for example. Culturally relevant teaching, according to Ladson-Billings' framework, has three guiding principles and ensures students will:

1. experience academic success;
2. develop and maintain cultural competence; and
3. develop a critical consciousness by challenging the status quo and current social order.

Making these principles broad, educational goals means you have three goals—to help students (1) experience academic success (2) develop and maintain cultural competence, and (3) develop a critical consciousness. These are broad goals because you may not achieve them overnight; to achieve the goals, you will have to create specific objectives and design instructional activities around those objectives.

To illustrate, I will use the goals and objectives a colleague and I created for her unit on the Harlem Renaissance. We used the three principles listed above (Ladson-Billings, 1995) as our overall, broad goals. We created the following measurable, specific objectives, based on those goals.

By the end of this lesson, all students will

1. describe in writing 1-3 facts about the Harlem Renaissance as described in the video, *The Harlem Renaissance*.

2. list three different kinds of "Black art" that emerged from the Harlem Renaissance, as described in the video, *The Harlem Renaissance*.

3. (a) describe at least one barrier that African American artists experienced before the Harlem Renaissance, and (b) using no more than one paragraph, write freely about their opinion on injustice.

The first specific and measurable objective pertains to helping students achieve success—ensuring that they are learning. Our goal is to help students achieve throughout the school year, but the objective is based on the specific lesson you are designing, aligned with the principles you selected from the framework you adopted and your students' lived experiences. In the example above, students *learned* about the Harlem Renaissance, and we measured their learning using authentic assessments developed from the lesson.

The second specific and measurable objective pertains to developing cultural competence; the teacher included activities related to "Black art." Students recalled various art forms as described in the video, *The Harlem Renaissance*, students also demonstrated the *Lindy Hop* and *Charleston* dances and learned how the Harlem Renaissance influenced pop culture, including hip-hop. Students then created choreography that depicted the evolution of dance, describing the similarities and differences between dances during the Harlem Renaissance era and dances from their cultures, including "hip-hop dance," as described by a student leader.

The third specific and measurable objective pertains to developing a critical consciousness. The teacher I coached started this process by exploring how her students felt about injustice. She and her students then critiqued injustice that occurred before and during the Harlem Renaissance; they concluded the lesson by critiquing injustice that occurs in society today. Considering critical consciousness is associated with challenging the status quo, the question becomes, what will you and your students challenge in your lesson, and how will you do it?

As illustrated in the example above, culturally responsive teaching is applying frameworks and principles. If you are using Ladson-Billings' framework, the question becomes, how will you ensure that students will *achieve academic success*? How will you ensure they *maintain cultural competence and academic excellence* in your classroom? How will you ensure they *develop critical consciousness* to learn skills to challenge the status quo? Constructing specific, measurable goals help address these questions.

Turning principles into lesson objectives will ensure that your instructional practices are culturally meaningful. Essentially, when applying frameworks, the question is, What instructional activities will you employ to achieve your goals? This question is crucial because it helps you think through the guiding principles, and it gives you, the designer, autonomy to design based on your teaching preferences, your students' values, and your knowledge of cultural values and community practices (which, again, you learned from The Big Four).

Considering practitioners found these tips useful, I will include videos and templates in our Redesign private Facebook group. You can use them as examples to create goals and objectives based on the framework you select to guide your design. When you use templates designed from culturally meaningful principles, you can return to the template and the culturally meaningful framework to show stakeholders how and why your practices are student-centered, culturally meaningful, and equitable based on your students' interests. When you do this, I recommend focusing on each framework's guiding principles. Here is how you can do it:

1. explain that culturally responsive teaching is applying a culturally meaningful framework;
2. explain the cultural framework you selected to guide your study;
3. state and describe the principles that comprise the frameworks;

4. define what each principle means and describe how you created goals and objectives from the principles; and

5. use student narratives or student-response handouts to illustrate how students met the lesson's goals.

Here is the process we took through the 7-week training that led to applying frameworks to design culturally meaningful activities.

1. ***Problem Identification***: We started the study by identifying problems (challenges/barriers) that prevented practitioners from designing culturally responsive practices.

2. ***Problem Exploration:*** Then, we explored those problems to determine which ones we could transform within the 7-week training session.

3. ***Problem Transformation:*** Finally, we searched for and co-designed tools specifically related to the problems we selected to transform, and we employed those tools to design culturally meaningful SEL activities.

I started the study by hosting a focus group, where practitioners spent the entire session identifying and exploring problems that prevented them from designing culturally responsive practices. After this, I analyzed their descriptions of problems from that meeting, and I placed their problems into categories (see Chapter 2 to review these categories). Practitioners described 117 problems during that meeting; more than half were problems related to lacking knowledge of culturally responsive teaching. I introduced *The LEARN Framework for Practice* to address the lack of knowledge of culturally responsive teaching, and here is how I did it.

L—Learn The Big Four

First, I introduced the *L* component of the framework, in which I engaged practitioners in a host of activities related to *The Big Four. The Big Four* addressed most of their problems related to lacking knowledge of culturally responsive teaching.

E—Examine Thoughts, Beliefs, and Attitudes Related to The Big Four

Second, I engaged practitioners in activities to create opportunities for them to examine their thoughts, beliefs, and attitudes related to *The Big Four*. During this component of the framework, practitioners reflected on the history of culturally responsive education (CRE), cultural values, and community practices. They also reflected on their cultural values (i.e., how their cultural values guided their practices and how their values clashed with their students' values in the classroom).

A—Adopt/Apply a Culturally Meaningful Framework to Guide Designs

Finally, I reintroduced the three frameworks (from *The Big Four*), and I explained how to use them as guides to design culturally meaningful practices. I coached practitioners through converting guiding principles into goals and objectives to achieve in the classroom. I also taught them how to explain their activities to stakeholders using their culturally meaningful objectives, culturally meaningful frameworks, and culturally meaningful principles guiding the lesson activity.

In our Facebook group, *Redesign*, I illustrate "The Case of Karly" to give you an example of how practitioners applied frameworks during the study. Karly was a social worker who participated in the study to learn more about culturally responsive community-building activities. She understood the power of these activities and wanted to learn how to implement them in the classroom. She also wanted to show teachers how to create them to build community in their classrooms.

She started the study with the goal of "finding" culturally responsive curricula. She finished the study learning that culturally responsive teaching is not about "finding" pre-planned, pre-packaged, and prescriptive culturally responsive curricula. Instead, she learned that culturally responsive teaching is learning *The Big Four* and using specific tools from *The Big Four* to design culturally responsive practices. Finally, she went from searching for culturally responsive community-building activities and curricula to designing practices using a framework and her students' interests. Karly and I present her case in the *Redesign* private Facebook group. Be sure to join this group to learn about using culturally meaningful frameworks and principles to design culturally meaningful objectives.

Culturally Meaningful Practices and Activities

Remember, I use the phrase "culturally meaningful practices" to illustrate that the practices are meaningful according to a specific framework. For example, if you use Ladson-Billings' (1995) culturally relevant pedagogy to design activities, then your practices are meaningful based on her framework. To understand these practices, you must know her framework's three principles.

If you design culturally responsive activities according to Gay's (2014) framework, then your practices are meaningful and best understood within the context of her framework. Likewise, if you design culturally *sustaining* activities, your practices are meaningful according to, and best understood within the context of Paris's (2012) culturally sustaining pedagogy. During the study, when practitioners presented their designs, they stated whose framework they adopted and applied (letter *A*)—i.e., "I used Gay's framework, and here is how I did it . . . here is how my activity is culturally responsive . . ." They described how their activities were meaningful, according to their selected framework.

Explaining how their designs were culturally meaningful helped them understand that CRE comprises multiple theories, principles, and frameworks. It helped them understand that principles within a particular framework (Paris's culturally sustaining pedagogy, for example) have a specific meaning and that, to best understand the meaning and the designed lesson, it is necessary to understand the principles that activity is designed after. Thus, culturally meaningful practices suggest that practices have specific meanings and purposes. To understand the meaning and purpose, it is necessary to know the framework that gives it meaning.

Therefore, when you hear the phrase culturally meaningful practices, your next thought should be, "What do these practices *mean*?" Again, the meaning comes from the framework and guiding principles, so to answer the question of meaning, you need to know the framework and principles that guide the framework. Consider the following vignette to understand how I used culturally sustaining principles in practice—practices that are meaningful according to Paris's (2012) framework.

Culturally Sustaining Practices—a Vignette

As a school psychologist and interventionist, I provide an array of support and interventions in the classroom, and I co-design social and emotional learning (SEL) and trauma-informed groups with students. When I co-design these groups, I use culturally meaningful frameworks to design them. I don't necessarily need the *Culturally Meaningful Comparison Table* (see Tables 15 and 16) to guide me because I have memorized principles related to the three frameworks I introduced in this chapter, a process you will experience if you use the frameworks consistently.

When I co-design SEL groups with students, I draw from Paris's (2012) culturally *sustaining* pedagogy framework. If you observed my support groups and did not know about culturally sustaining principles, you would see students rapping, reciting poetry, singing, and dancing; you would notice that students learned SEL competencies and processed stress and trauma using the arts. If you were knowledgeable of the principles that comprise culturally sustaining pedagogy, however, you might quickly observe that I do not simply "use" their cultures and community practices to engage them instructionally.

If you knew *The Big Four*, you would know that culturally meaningful frameworks build from other frameworks. Thus, a vital goal of all culturally meaningful frameworks is to incorporate students' community practices, lived experiences, and cultural values with instruction. If you had knowledge of culturally sustaining pedagogy, however, you might notice that one of my goals in my hip-hop support groups is to sustain the languages, community practices, and social identities of my students. You might also predict that I might engage in activities that allow students to critique lyrics to determine if their favorite artist marginalizes groups of people in their music. From this perspective, employing the arts during instructional time is meaningful, according to Paris's (2012) descriptions of culturally sustaining pedagogy.

Bobby

During the 2021–2022 school year, I met a freshman student who raps, sings, and recites poetry. I'll call him Bobby. I have been facilitating *culturally meaningful*— i.e., culturally *relevant*, culturally *responsive*, and culturally *sustaining*—activities since 2012. Compared with all the other students I have worked with since 2012, Bobby was, by far, the most talented. Although he was already super confident and a leader in his own right, I made him a leader in our groups and created opportunities for him to engage with his gifts, talents, and abilities after school within his community.

By the end of the school year, we learned about a poetry slam happening about 40 miles away from his house. The event organizer was a community leader who wrote poetry to cope with life's challenges. She also wrote music and sang to shed light on and process her lived experiences. She invited my hip-hop group to participate in the poetry slam, which three of my students attended, including Bobby. Bobby stole the show, won the poetry slam, and became even more confident in his ability as an artist.

What do you suppose my goal was for Bobby instructionally? My goal was not to simply develop SEL or address trauma; instead, my goal was to use SEL competencies—including self-awareness, self-management, social awareness, relationship skills, and responsible decision-making—as tools to sustain Bobby's multiple identities, including his identities as an artist and as a young Black male who embraced African American Vernacular English. Considering my goal was to *sustain* his identities, three core goals were to sustain (1) positive views concerning

Black people in general and Black males in particular; (2) his ways of using language in creative ways; and (3) the practice of using rap and poetry as tools to process life.

Since I drew from Paris's (2012) framework, I can describe how my instructional practices were related to culturally sustaining principles; I can describe how my goals were tied to the principles associated with culturally responsive education; and I can measure whether my activities—i.e., culturally sustaining SEL activities, community events, including poetry slam—were effective at helping me achieve goals of sustaining his identities.

After the show, Bobby discussed how much he learned about himself from performing. He spoke of the many poets he met—all who offered to mentor him— and he said, "I can easily see how I can use my talents to help people deal with pain, and I can see how I can make money from these kinds of events." When we met in my office the next school day, I told him he and I would process the poetry slam "using social and emotional competencies." I told him I would name a competency and, based on the definition of the competency, I wanted him to describe his experiences at the poetry slam. Bobby was well prepared for this activity as he recited and defined all five competencies in seconds; students in our hip-hop group learned SEL in explicit ways, and Bobby often led an activity designed to help him and his peers learn all five competencies in a short amount of time.

I looked at him and said, "self-awareness." In response, Bobby described how he felt at the event. He described his anxiety level before performing and commented that his levels decreased while performing. He concluded that he was not anxious by the show's end. I said, "self-management," to which he responded, "Did you see me walking back and forth on stage as I was spittin'?" When I told him yes, he continued, "That's what I do when I get real anxious when I'm spittin'. I move around. It calms my nerves." I stated all five competencies to which Bobby responded, based on his experiences with the poetry slam.

The meaning of my practices in the vignette is found within the context of culturally sustaining pedagogy. My use of hip-hop, poetry, African American

Vernacular English (AAVE), and other practices have a specific purpose, meaning, and goal—and to understand what they are, you must know about culturally sustaining pedagogy. For example, return to Table 16 and read the definition and guiding principles of culturally sustaining pedagogy. Try to identify how my practices were meaningful according to culturally sustaining guiding principles.

This vignette exemplifies what we can do using culturally meaningful frameworks. Do you see how I can be intentional about my practices when using a culturally meaningful framework? Do you see how I can be intentional about my purpose for using culturally meaningful principles? I was intentional because I drew directly from a framework in purposeful ways. If teachers had asked, "Dwayne, can you share exactly how the poetry slam was culturally meaningful for Bobby?" I could do the following:

1. show educators the Culturally Meaningful Comparison Table (Table 15);
2. direct them to the culturally sustaining column;
3. share the definition on the table;
4. point to guiding principles; and
5. explain how my practices were culturally meaningful according to the framework principles.

Do these examples make sense? Have you had any aha moments? Notice how, in the above example, I can return to the principles and show how I applied them in my practice.

You might think, "I don't facilitate social and emotional learning or trauma-informed groups, so I cannot do any of this." If you thought this, I have good news for you: I use culturally responsive frameworks when working with teachers in their classrooms across subjects.

Usually, I help teachers design "community building" activities that are culturally meaningful, and I coach them through the process I shared with you in this section. I teach them that each culturally meaningful framework has a specific meaning based on the principles of the frameworks. To understand the meaning, it is necessary to know the principles that comprise the frameworks.

Culturally responsive teaching is learning *The Big Four* and *adopting/applying* a culturally meaningful framework to guide you as you design culturally meaningful activities. Throughout this book, I commented that it is impossible to design culturally meaningful activities—i.e., culturally *relevant, responsive, sustaining, and others*—intentionally if you are unfamiliar with culturally meaningful frameworks. The key in that sentence is "intentionally." How do you design something intentionally that you are unfamiliar with?

If you have never learned about culturally meaningful frameworks and are unfamiliar with the principles that compose the frameworks, then how will you use those principles to guide your practice? You can't, which is why, to design culturally meaningful practices intentionally, you must first learn about *The Big Four* and then use knowledge and insight gained from *The Big Four* to organize activities in culturally *meaningful* ways.

Summary

In this chapter, I introduced the letter *A* of *The LEARN Framework*. Letter *A* of the framework stands for *adopt/apply* a framework. After learning about and examining *The Big Four* (letters L and E), the next step is to *adopt/apply* a framework to guide you as you design culturally responsive activities. I showed you how to adopt and apply a framework and convert culturally meaningful principles into learning objectives, and I shared how you can defend your practice by showing how and why it is culturally meaningful based on your students' experiences.

What's Next?

In the next section, I discuss the letter *R* of *The LEARN Framework*, which stands for reflection, and I discuss the importance of reflecting on your designed practices to identify areas requiring iterations.

Chapter 12:

R—Reflect

... for me, it was the combination of the last phase of [the training] honestly [that made things click]. But for me, it was really the reflection portion of this last phase, like I had done what I thought was kind of the triangle [an analytical tool and design template], but it was our conversations . . . talking about 'How am I doing this like that' [explaining how the design was culturally responsive]. That's what it boils down to like knowing your framework, looking at what you do on a regular basis, and asking how am I doing this [how am I applying principles]? Yeah. And if you can't come up with a response, then you're not doing it. And just, you know, just in my mind, I feel like there's so much potential moving into next year with our [equity work, using this information].

—PhD Research Participant

How often do you reflect on your practices after implementing classroom activities? Do you ever reflect on which students were engaged and which ones were not? Do you reflect on the rules you created to govern the activities to determine if they were insensitive to the cultural values and community practices of students who participated in the activity? How about the division of labor? How often do you reflect on who does what during instructional time to determine if you and your students share power and voice in the classroom? Do you create opportunities to co-plan, co-design, and co-facilitate lessons with students? Are you the purveyor of knowledge in the classroom? Do you perceive students as docile learners?

In this chapter, I introduce the letter *R* of *The LEARN Framework for Practice*, which stands for *Reflect*. By the end of this chapter, you will be able to:

- reflect on specific elements of your lesson plans to improve their designs, using a culturally meaningful tool;
- reflect on which cultural values dominate your classroom practices;
- reflect on how your cultural values show up in your classroom activities;
- reflect on whether you and your students are experiencing cultural clashes in the classroom; and
- reflect on whether your instructional approach and classroom expectations create *cultural harmony*—respecting cultural values, lived experiences, and community practices—or *cultural disharmony*—disrespecting and marginalizing specific cultural values, lived experiences, and community practices.

Thus far, we've *learned* (L) about and *examined* (E) *The Big Four*, and we've learned how to *adopt* and *apply* (A) a framework to guide us as we design culturally meaningful activities. After we design activities, using knowledge of *The Big Four* and applying a framework to guide our designs, we must reflect on whether our designed activities engage students in the classroom. We must reflect on aspects of the activity that require improvement. In this section, I explain the importance of reflection and provide a tool to guide you as you reflect on the activity you will design. Using the tool, practitioners in my study reflected on six elements of their activities, and they reflected on how they might change their practices based on what they learned from reflection.

Reflection

When you think of the term reflection, what comes to your mind? How do you define it? Reflection is a mental activity by which we concentrate on instances of our lived experiences. We recall and direct our attention to events, tools, interactions, and other things we experience in our environments. The letter *R* of *The LEARN Framework* is reflecting on your designed activity while focusing on specific elements related to the cultural-historical activity theory (CHAT) framework. I coached practitioners on these elements, and they described that understanding the activity elements helped them analyze and critique their instructional practices; they described the elements as useful for designing meaningful practices, and they used the elements to guide them as they reflected on their designed activities.

In what follows, I discuss the CHAT framework, which includes six elements of your instructional designs, and I include an image to help you visualize the importance of each component. Understanding the six elements will provide insight into why some students engage and some disengage. I also discuss how the elements contribute to teacher-student relationships and disciplining and referring students of color for special education services at disproportionate rates compared with White students. You can use what you learn in this book to re-imagine each activity element to make your practices culturally meaningful.

Reflecting on the six elements I include in this chapter will help you consider how students responded to your design activities. It provides an opportunity for you to analyze and critique your activity so you can learn of potential cultural clashes during instructional time.

Cultural Historical Activity Theory

CHAT is a framework that offers tools to analyze and reflect on professional practice, including instructional activities in the classroom. CHAT is rooted in decades of research, originating with Russian psychologist Lev Vygotsky's ideas on tool use and mediation (see Chapter 1 for a discussion on mediation). The framework is commonly used to analyze and describe human activities and interactions within learning environments (Yamagata-Lynch, 2010).

Although CHAT is rooted in decades of research, I will not explain the theory exhaustively. Instead, I will explain how practitioners and I used the framework in my research study and how you can use it as a tool to analyze and reflect on your designed practices. I introduce CHAT by first defining what each word in the phrase "cultural-historical activity theory" means so you can understand its relationship to culturally meaningful practices. Then I discuss six elements of the framework that guided the work of practitioners in my study—six features you can use to reflect on your lessons to determine if you should adjust your practices based on the cultural needs of your students. Finally, I conclude this discussion by addressing the implications of using CHAT when designing culturally meaningful practices and reflecting on instructional activities.

CHAT—the Meaning is in The Framework

Throughout this book, I have stated that all frameworks have meaning and shared that the meaning is within the framework. CHAT is no different. Each word in the name "cultural-historical activity theory" has a particular meaning. I have found that pairing CHAT with culturally meaningful frameworks has been the most effective way of designing practices and reflecting on those activities. Teachers in my study were amazed at what they could do using the framework.

Cultural

What do you think the word cultural means within the context of CHAT? The word *cultural* in the phrase *cultural-historical activity theory* highlights the impact of culture on our daily lives. CHAT acknowledges that our cultural experiences influence our worldviews. From this perspective, we:

- engage through culture;

- form identities through culture;

- develop and maintain relationships through culture;

- construct rules and expectations through culture;

- process pain through culture;

- determine what is good and bad through culture—and so on.

CHAT acknowledges that cultural values and perspectives shape professional practices, including educational instructional practices, rules, and expectations in the classroom.

In American schools, for example, policies, norms, expectations, and practices often align with Eurocentric, mainstream cultural values, the same values I discussed in Chapter 9 as part of *The Big Four*. Students experience cultural clashes when they enter spaces and demonstrate behaviors different from mainstream culture's values. This difference often creates classroom tension, resulting in student disengagement and poor teacher-student relationships. I call this tension "cultural clashes," and I define clashes as instances in which cultural values collide in the classroom and create educational environments that inhibit learning.

Cultural clashes are one reason teachers refer and qualify students of color for special education services at disproportionate rates compared to White students. Here is how it happens. Because of cultural clashes, many students disengage during instructional time. Students miss instruction when they disengage, and when they miss instruction over time, they perform below standards; sometimes they perform as if they have a range of learning disabilities because of the many hours of instruction missed due to disengagement. When students don't respond positively to instruction and interventions over time, we refer and qualify them for special education services. Students are given punitive consequences and learning disability labels at alarming rates in response to cultural clashes in the classroom.

CHAT's emphasis on culture acknowledges that culture mediates learning, interactions, engagement, and other factors critical to achieving at a high level in the classroom. Reflecting on the cultural elements of your designed practices then, which I will show you how to do in this chapter, creates an opportunity for you to analyze your practices in ways that center on culture and its impact on teaching, learning, and relationships.

Historical

What do you think the word *historical* means within the context of CHAT? It refers to our being a part of history, connected in meaningful ways to events that have occurred throughout our life and events within the world in general. From this perspective, CHAT framework and theories suggest that we are connected to and influenced by our histories. This means our histories, our experiences, influence how we perceive the world, engage with others, and interpret phenomena.

Unlike focusing on the "here and now," commonly taught in counseling programs, CHAT perspectives trace experiences and connect individuals to their histories to understand events—and how the past now affects present life. Reflecting on history helps us know that what we observe in the classroom may be rooted in the history of a student's life. Often, if those issues are not addressed, students may disengage in the classroom and have poor educational experiences. History also pertains to how we make decisions as educators. For example, we may engage in particular practices or refuse to engage in them based on our histories— things that have shaped our beliefs and attitudes throughout our development.

History explains why students of color make claims about racism and become frustrated when they do not have opportunities to read books that praise and honor African Americans for their contributions; it explains why some students of color shut down and disengage when they read books that use the N-word in their classes.

Activity

What do you think the word *activity* means within the context of CHAT? Activity refers to collective actions and interactions of people, influenced by history and culture, within a particular context. In my book, *Redesign: An SEL Toolkit to Designing Culturally Sustaining and Antiracist Practices* (Williams, 2020), I describe activity like this:

> Within any organization, team members engage in specific actions to accomplish short- and long-term goals. According to CHAT, activity refers to all actions and interactions that team members engage in to accomplish a task (Engestrom, 2001); stated differently, group members' interaction and collective actions to achieve a task refer to an activity. Stakeholders, including students, parents, practitioners, administrators, and community members, interact within "activity systems" (p. 135) to provide students with the highest level of instruction. In activity systems, activity members construct rules, use cultural tools to teach and process relevant content, and devise goals for the system. However, goals may shift based on the needs of activity members and the system.

> School-based "activity systems" include general and special education classrooms, counseling groups—including social and emotional learning and trauma-informed groups—restorative circles, multi-tiered system of supports—which teachers often refer to by the initials, calling them MTSS—problem-solving teams, special education evaluation and eligibility teams, and so on. CHAT principles contend that all activity systems (all classrooms, groups, and teams where people interact in schools) are rooted in culture, considering activity systems comprise cultural group members who interact, share perspectives, and design, based on cultural worldviews.

The problem in most schools is that although activity systems comprise racially and culturally diverse members, instructional strategies, tools, rules, perspectives, and ways of being are often rooted in Eurocentric values, principles, and ways of thinking.

CHAT offers practitioners tools to analyze and reflect on their designed practices.

Theory

What do you think the word *theory* means within the context of CHAT? Theory refers to concepts and principles individuals can use to understand, guide, and describe phenomena. CHAT is a practitioner-based framework that leads to designing and redesigning work-related activities, and it offers tools to analyze challenges within work-related practices; it provides tools to resolve those challenges to design and redesign activities based on the needs of activity members—individuals who interact within a particular system such as a learning environment (Williams, 2020).

Using CHAT as a Reflection Tool

Now that you understand what each word means in the phrase cultural-historical activity theory, I will focus on six of CHAT's elements and show you how you can use them as a guide to reflect on your practices.

These elements include:

1. participants
2. tools
3. object
4. community
5. expectations
6. roles

Scholars who write about CHAT use the word "subjects" instead of participants, "division of labor" instead of roles, and "rules" instead of expectations. In this book, I use "participants" instead of subjects, "roles" instead of division of labor, and "expectations" instead of rules.

The activity system as a collective is the unit of analysis within CHAT. This means that all six elements are understood as one unit; any new changes in the unit—any new change in any of the six elements—can change how the entire unit functions. Therefore, when using the CHAT framework to analyze practices, you would analyze practices as a collective and seek to understand how system elements affect one another. This starkly contrasts with isolating elements within the system and studying each element individually.

From this perspective, all elements in this unit—for example, participants, tools, object, and so on—affect each other in significant ways, and history and culture are driving forces in the system. In Figure 8, I illustrate the familiar triangle CHAT scholars use to describe the nature of activity systems. Following the triangle, I show you how each element affects the other in this system. Note that the triangle in Figure 8 uses the words "subject," "rules," and "division of labor." Remember, my terms—participants, expectations, and labor—mean the same thing as subjects, rules, and division of labor. In Figure 8, I use the terms most scholars use when explaining CHAT just in case you want to Google the framework to learn more about CHAT's elements.

Figure 8: CHAT Triangle

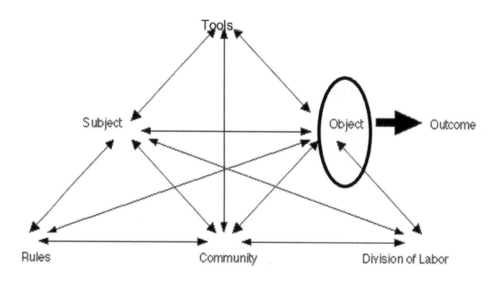

According to CHAT, all six elements—subject [participants], tools, object, rules [expectations], community, and division of labor [labor]—impact each other, which is why the image includes bi-directional lines. *Subject* refers to all individuals involved in the activity system. As for K-12 education, subjects include students and teachers engaged in teaching and learning. *Tools* include social others, cultural values, physical resources—including books, computers, pencils, paper, and an array of other artifacts we use to aid teaching and learning—and background knowledge.

The *object* motivates the activity; it is what brings individuals together for some cause. I often give the example of facilitating trauma-informed groups for students who have experienced traumatic events. Many students have experienced trauma that impacts their ability to do well in the classroom. Therefore, there is a *need* to create trauma-informed support groups—activity systems—to help students learn tools and strategies to process trauma in and out of school. This need motivates my colleagues and me to design lessons to help students learn skills to process trauma. However, our purpose or motivation for these groups may change over time because of a new need or purpose. Therefore, the object is the reason the activity exists, and everything within the activity is organized around the object to fulfill the identified need—the goal. To give you an example, the object for my trauma-informed groups was the need to design culturally meaningful trauma-informed programming so students could process traumatic events and learn skills to deal with their experiences.

I will not go into detail in this book about *outcomes*. However, I give multiple examples of outcomes in the *Redesign* Facebook group. In this book, think of outcomes as generalizing learning from one setting to another; it is performing a new skill in multiple settings. For example, the object of an activity might be related to developing self-management skills to process stress and trauma. The *outcome*, based on this object—the motivation for the activity—refers to students learning self-management skills in school *and* using them at home and within their communities (or other settings). Again, I will not go into detail about outcomes in this book. However, remember that it refers to generalizing learning from one setting to another.

As you might expect, *rules* are formal and informal expectations that students and teachers create to have the best opportunity to achieve the goal of the activity, the object. The community includes all individuals involved in helping the subjects accomplish the goal of the activity system; in the classroom, the community consists of all individuals invested in helping students and teachers achieve their desired goals. *Division* of *Labor* refers to how tasks are divided and shared among subjects to accomplish the object, the goal of the activity. The outcome of an *activity* results from subjects acting on the object collectively, using other elements—such as tools, rules, and division of labor—to achieve the desired result or goal of the activity system.

During the 7-week training session, practitioners used the CHAT framework to design and reflect on their designs. From a CHAT perspective, they kept their *students* in mind as they designed their practices; they reflected on the *tools* they included in their designs; they reflected on the *object* (purpose/goal) of their lessons, what they hoped to accomplish with their designs, and how their designs were culturally meaningful; they reflected on *community* members involved in the learning process, and they contemplated on whom they should invite into their activity system—their learning environment—based on the needs of students.

They also reflected on how they planned to divide the labor during instructional time and what they hoped to accomplish as an outcome of the activity. Practitioners reflected on how students might use the learning from the activity to enhance racial and cultural identity and challenge the status quo. Remember that I did not include students as participants in my study; therefore, although practitioners used tools they co-designed in their classrooms right away, I could not analyze how they used tools or how their students responded to them because students were not a part of the study.

Since practitioners could not reflect on how students responded to the designed activity—because students were not a part of the study—practitioners reflected on how they designed their activities based on each element. Therefore, when you design your practices, it will be important for you to reflect on the elements as teachers did in my study, but it will also be vital that you reflect on whether your activity was effective at engaging students and achieving the purpose of designing the activity (object).

In the next section, I conclude the chapter by providing a list of questions you can use as a guide when reflecting on culturally meaningful practices using the CHAT framework. They are the same questions that practitioners reflected on as they designed and analyzed practices during my research study.

Questions to Guide Your Reflection on Designed Activities

Following are guiding questions you can use to reflect on your designed practices. Practitioners in my study used the questions to analyze, critique, and problematize their instructional practices. Then, after designing culturally meaningful activities, they used the same questions to reflect on their designs. The following are reflection questions for each of CHAT's six elements

Subjects: Who are the students and teachers involved in this activity lesson?

- In what ways did the values of teachers influence the activity?
- In what ways did the values of students influence the activity?

Object: What was the motivation for this designed activity? What was the need or purpose?

- What need did you identify and work to address?

Tools: What tools did you use to design interventions?

- Why did you use those tools?
- Were they the most appropriate tools based on your students' cultural needs?
- How did students respond to those tools?

Rules: What rules governed your designed activity?

- Were rules rooted in your cultural values, the values of students, or a combination of both?
- How might you create rules closely related to your students' cultural values next time?

Community: Who were the community members helping you and your students achieve goals?

- How did you include them within the designed activity?
- How did they help you achieve the goal of your design?

Division of Labor: How did you divide tasks in your designed activity?

- Why did you divide the tasks among each participant the way you did?
- Is the activity multi-voiced, by which everyone in the learning task has a voice in the design of the activity?
- Which of your students did not engage during the activity, and why didn't they?

There you have it! You now have knowledge related to the basic tenets of CHAT, and you can use this framework as a tool to design, analyze, critique, and problematize practices. I have taught teachers, administrators, and students how to use this model. Students and I have used the framework to co-design activities, in which we designed SEL activities using the arts, including spoken word, hip-hop, and dance. I have also used the framework to design and reflect on community-building activities for the general education classroom. CHAT is my go-to framework when I analyze practices. Although CHAT scholars do not use the framework to design lesson activities, I use the framework as both an analytical tool and a design template to organize my thoughts on how I might co-design activities for and with students.

In this section, I provided the basic tenets of CHAT. Previously I shared that I created a private Facebook group so you and all other readers can support each other as you learn about culturally meaningful teaching and design culturally meaningful practices. I include additional resources on the CHAT framework in the private group, including videos that show you step-by-step how to use the framework to analyze, problematize, and re-imagine your current practices. Therefore, if you want to use the CHAT framework to redesign your practices in culturally meaningful ways, be sure to join the private group. Search *Redesign* to join us!

Summary

In this chapter, I introduced the letter *R* of *The LEARN Framework*. I introduced the CHAT framework as a tool you can use to reflect on current and designed practices. I defined activity systems, and you learned about the six elements that comprise activity systems: participants/subjects, tools, object(s), community, rules, and division of labor/roles.

What's Next?

Thus far, you have *learned* about *The Big Four* (*L*); you *examined The Big Four* (*E*); you *adopted/applied* a framework (*A*), and in this chapter, you learned about a tool to use to guide your *reflection* (*R*) on designed activities. In the next chapter, I discuss the final letter of *The LEARN Framework*, the letter *N*, which stands for *negotiate*. I discuss best practices for negotiating the curriculum with your students.

Chapter 13:

N—Negotiate

I am using values that students identified prior to the session and incorporating these into the session. I am using the funds of knowledge [tool practitioners and I co-designed] to understand the values of students. I am also sustaining their culture by using cultural values [drawing from Paris's 2012 framework principles] throughout the entire session. I would also want to be mindful of how my race could impact students' comfort level especially in discussing trauma and because many of the students identified racial violence and police brutality as things that concern them [drawing from Gay's 2014 framework principles]. I would want my students to know my beliefs and for them to have already had open dialogue with me by the time we get to this session about police brutality and racial violence [drawing from Ladson-Billings' 1995 framework principles]. I would not want students to get to this session unsure of where I stand and how I feel, and I would not want them to feel they need to edit themselves [drawing from all three frameworks].

—PhD Research Participant

How often do you create opportunities for students to co-plan, co-design, and co-facilitate activities in the classroom? How often do you negotiate with students about how they want to learn academic content? Do you think it is necessary to negotiate with students when designing activities?

In this chapter, I introduce the letter *N* of *The LEARN Framework for Practice,* which stands for *negotiate.* By the end of this chapter, you will be able to:

- articulate the importance of negotiating your curriculum, including your syllabi, with students when designing culturally meaningful practices;
- negotiate your curriculum with students;
- employ a culturally meaningful tool to guide as you negotiate your curriculum with students; and
- describe common pitfalls when negotiating curricula and explain how to respond to them in practice.

I begin by sharing a story I included in the *Introduction* section of my PhD dissertation. The story illustrates a time when a group of Black students expressed frustration about reading books with the word "nigger" in their English classes. I explain how this experience changed the purpose of my SEL support groups. Instead of sticking to what I had planned for that semester, I negotiated with students and co-planned activities to critique and challenge the status quo in their schools.

I share this story to illustrate the power of negotiated learning and describe the benefits of negotiating the syllabus and curriculum with students. I describe how you can use CHAT's six elements (see Chapter 12) as a tool for negotiating. I conclude by discussing the challenges I have experienced with negotiated learning. I provide tips on resolving the challenges you might encounter when negotiating with students in your classroom.

How About We Write About This Racist Ass School

During the 2019–2020 school year, months before Illinois Governor J.B. Pritzker announced the COVID-19 shelter-in-place mandates, I worked with students to organize a "hip-hop" social and emotional learning (SEL) counseling group at a high school in the Midwest U.S.A. Students and I met once a week for 50 minutes, and students ended each session by selecting social and emotional competencies (SECs) they wanted to discuss in the next session. In addition to selecting SECs, students established rules for the following session, and they passed around an "order of performance" sign-up form that listed the order in which they would perform their SEC content. Activities included rap battles, dance battles, singing, and poetry. Students naturally drew from their cultural values, lived experiences, and community practices when processing and demonstrating their knowledge and understanding of SECs.

After a lengthy discussion on the rules to follow and competency to process for the next session, students decided to discuss the SEC *social awareness*. Based on this competency, I suggested an idea: "So y'all are going to write about social awareness? That's what's up! I have an idea. I think it would be dope if y'all write about how y'all experience America as youth of color. Y'all could write about what it is like to be a youth of color in America." During group sessions, I often suggested ideas that students laughed at, modified, or rejected.

One of the group members immediately chimed in, in response to my comment. Her words triggered an uproar and students jumped from their seats, clapped their hands, and dapped each other up. "Nah, Mr. Williams," the student shouted. "How about we write about our experiences in this racist ass school?" She then leaped from her chair and landed in the center of the group's circle, where she addressed her group members. "Y'all wanna write about social awareness . . . about what we see in this school . . . about what we experience as Black youth in this school? Y'all wanna write about what we read every day in these got damn books? What we see in the videos teachers show? Yeah, we gonna address social awareness, alright. We gonna address our experiences—what we see and deal with in this racist ass school!"

As she spoke, another student interrupted her. " . . . Yeah, and when we write, we gotta keep it all the way one-hundred! Talk about what y'all see, hear, and experience in this school as Black people."

The hip-hop SEL groups became the most popular counseling groups in the building among students who embraced hip-hop, and colleagues often requested to observe the group to learn how to incorporate hip-hop principles into their counseling groups. The students and I invited one of my colleagues to join our next session, the session on social awareness. During the session, students read lyrics and poetry from their phones about experiencing racism, discrimination, and injustice within their school. In addition, students gave presentations about being "tired" of reading books like *To Kill A Mockingbird.*

As for this book, students expressed that they were tired of hearing White teachers and White students say "nigger" throughout the class period; they were tired of hearing the audio rendition of the word played through the classroom speakers. Students lamented that reading these texts in class was most frustrating and awkward, especially when they were the only Black student in those spaces. The SEL group session transitioned into a discussion on resisting oppression.

One member led a discussion on the topic "resistance," and group members brainstormed how they could use social and emotional competencies as tools to resist oppression in their schools and within society. Finally, students identified trusted adults in the building to discuss and process perceived racism. They called these educators "White allies," White teachers dedicated to social justice. And we talked about the benefits of sharing racial experiences with trusted educators in the building. We concluded this session with breathing techniques.

When this SEL group session ended, as my students exited the classroom, my colleague commented, "Wow, Dwayne. I didn't expect this. I came in hoping to get some ideas to incorporate into my groups, but I could never recreate something like that. I could never see myself running a group like that. I wouldn't feel comfortable taking back any of this to my groups. I don't think I would be able to design a group that addresses the experiences of Black students as you all did." She also commented on the hip-hop instrumental music I played in the background as the students entered the room: "If I were to play hip-hop instrumental music in the background during a group with all Black kids, I'd feel silly. I'm sure the kids would laugh at me. I'd feel that I was misappropriating hip-hop culture."

My colleague acknowledged a valid point; it is true that she probably could not recreate the same experience that my students and I created, and here is why. Our group sessions were a mixture of personalities, identities, cultural values, desires, passions, and lived experiences; sessions reflected students' accomplishments, talents, abilities, creativity, pain, and frustration. Ultimately, our group sessions reflected students' desire to challenge the status quo based on the narratives they shared.

For a moment, let's use the CHAT triangle I showed you in the previous chapter to visualize the activity that students and I negotiated, co-planned, co-designed, and co-facilitated. For review, let's have you complete the CHAT triangle based on my story about my students, how they became frustrated about using the N-word in their English classes, and how we designed an activity to address the experience. I will share a blank triangle, and I want you to return to the story; using that information, jot down the six elements you can draw from the story.

Figure 9: Analyzing Activities from a CHAT Lens

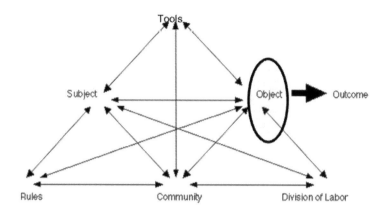

Use Figure 9 to document subjects/participants, tools, object, rules, community, and division of labor.

Subjects:

_____

_____

_____

_____

Tools:

_____

_____

_____

Object(s):

Rules:

Community:

_____

_____

_____

_____

_____

Division of Labor:

_____

_____

_____

_____

_____

As discussed in the previous chapter, CHAT is a tool we can use to analyze and reflect on our practices. I will use the framework to describe the lesson my students and I designed to address using the N-word in their English class. I will use that illustration to explain how you can negotiate the curriculum and learning.

Negotiated Curriculum and Learning

When students commented they were tired of reading books that included the N-word, I thanked them for bringing their frustrations to the support group to process their experiences. I told them we could talk about it, but that we were not going to simply talk in this group, but that we would aim to change the system. I asked them how we could make change in the building regarding reading books in the classroom that used the N-word, at which point students—who were all poets and dancers—shared they wanted to create poetry, PowerPoint slides, and narratives of their experiences in the next session. They then shared that, after using that session to process and share experiences about their English classes, they wanted to meet with administrators to share their experiences.

In response to the students' narratives, the building principal convened a meeting in the auditorium, where all teachers met. She talked about students' concerns. Eventually, teachers and administrators determined that they would no longer assign or read books in the English department that used the N-word, considering students also read books in their history classes that used the N-word, which was the students' main argument. They questioned why they could not read positive books about Black people during English, considering their history activities were filled with racial pain. The following includes how the six elements played out in that lesson.

Participants/Subjects: teachers and students

During the 2019–2020 school year, I co-designed six SEL support groups, including groups where students processed SEL by rapping, dancing, singing, and drawing. Each group included between 6 and 10 students. Students in these groups asked about "combining groups," in which all groups come together to process SEL by sharing their narratives and art. Students called these groups "Big Groups."

The social awareness session, where we addressed the N-word, was a "Big Group," comprised of 23 students. All students were African American males and females, except for one Hispanic female student. "Big Groups" included freshmen through senior students. Some students grew up in Chicago, while others grew up in Chicago's suburbs. All students valued activities that included communalism, movement expressiveness, orality, verve, and affection when processing SEL.

Object: motivation for the activity—the reason for the activity

The motivation for designing the social awareness activity was to process students' lived experiences with reading books that included the N-word and to identify how to address this concern as a collective.

Tools

To achieve the goal of this session, we included these tools:

- a Bluetooth wireless speaker
- a computer
- a projector
- narratives of lived experiences
- pencils
- paper
- instrumental hip-hop beats, among other tools

Tools also included cultural values, including communalism, movement expressiveness, orality, verve, and affect. These tools mediated teaching and learning, making it possible to achieve our goal.

Community

The community included "White Allies," including teachers, deans, and counselors dedicated to designing culturally meaningful practices and preparing students to challenge the status quo.

Rules/Expectations

Students and I negotiated rules for the social awareness activity. We agreed on these three rules:

1. confidentiality
2. respect each other, including performances and narratives
3. support each other

Confidentiality referred to "What is said in group stays in group." *Respect* included giving group members undivided attention during performances, which meant putting phones on silent (and sometimes out of sight) and ensuring conversations related to the group discussion. Support for each other included "clapping it up" for students after they shared performances. After a performance, students praised their peers by clapping and snapping their fingers.

Division of Labor

All students in the group had a role in the session. I started the meeting by thanking all students for showing up, briefly summarizing what to expect, and introducing the MC of the session. The MC introduced all the performers, and the performers either rapped, sang, shared stories, or recited poetry on their experiences related to reading books that used the N-word in their English classes. Students who did not perform chimed in by sharing their experiences in response to spoken word performances, and they praised their peers for performing. All members had the role of identifying a solution to reading books that used the N-word. Students wanted to meet with their teachers and administrators to describe how using the N-word made them feel.

Tying it all Together

The vignette in this chapter illustrates the letter *N* of *The LEARN Framework for Practice*. Students and I negotiated the syllabus and curriculum by co-planning, co-designing, and co-leading activities in our SEL support group. I did not perceive myself as a purveyor of knowledge or the sage on the stage, and I did not consider my students as passive learners who should hold tight to every word I spoke during instructional time. No—we were all teachers and learners; we created a "multi-voiced" learning environment where we shared power and co-designed lessons.

Negotiate, within *The LEARN Framework*, means negotiating the syllabus and curriculum. Teachers and students can negotiate tools, rules, objects, and division of labor, among other curricular elements, when designing activities. This contrasts with teachers planning activities by themselves or with other teachers, then delivering the lesson when students show up in the classroom. The difference in these approaches is that, with negotiation, students act agentically by participating in their learning. In what follows, I will share ideas on how you can negotiate in your classroom, no matter your content subject area.

Negotiating With Students Based on Your Content Area

Although I used the example of my hip-hop group, I have coached teachers across subjects on how to negotiate the syllabus and curriculum with students. Negotiating the syllabus creates opportunities for students to negotiate their assignments, including whether they will have group projects or work individually. Teachers and students can negotiate behavioral expectations and determine as a collective what should happen if students fail to meet expectations. I have coached educators on two approaches to negotiation, which I often use.

In the first approach, educators create a prototype design of their culturally meaningful activity and embed room for negotiation; then, they introduce the activity to students. The students' role in the process is to determine if the prototype activity appears engaging. Students will review the activity and provide meaningful feedback about the specific elements of the activity. For example, they may evaluate the activity and provide suggestions about the rules, tools, or division of labor. Collectively, the teacher(s) and students iterate the activity based on the group's feedback.

The second approach is to co-design with students from the start of the design process. With this approach, teachers and students discuss learning topics or some need, and collectively, they discuss potential activities related to the topic or their needs. This is what four practitioners and I did to design the online crash course we used during the research study.

I collaborated with four teachers to create a prototype course. When I started the research study, I introduced the prototype to educators who participated; we kept some elements of the prototype, removed others, and included additional features based on their needs. I use both approaches regularly when I design activities, and I have found them both effective at creating opportunities for students to participate in developing their lessons in the classroom.

This book introduces *The LEARN Framework for Practice* as a tool to design culturally meaningful practices. It is outside the scope of this book to describe the many ways you can negotiate your syllabus and curriculum in the classroom to create opportunities for student agency. If you are interested in additional resources related to negotiation, then I highly encourage you to join the private Facebook group and access the online curriculum, as these resources include greater detail and additional resources related to negotiated learning. Enroll in *The LEARN Academy* if you want to take a deeper dive into culturally meaningful teaching and personal coaching sessions from me on this topic.

Although it is outside the scope of this book to go into detail about negotiating your curriculum with students, the following are guiding questions you can use to think about the process:

- What *tools/resources* will I use to achieve my goal for my designed activity? How did I negotiate tools with students?
- What *rules* or expectations will I adopt to govern the instructional activity? How did I negotiate rules with students?
- What is the *object* or goal of my activity? What was my motivation for designing this activity? How did I negotiate the object with students?
- Who are the *community* members? How did I negotiate this with students?

- How did I divide the labor? Who is doing what? How was this negotiated with students?

The letter *N* within *The LEARN Framework* requires that educators embed opportunities for negotiation about tools, rules, object, community, and division of labor when designing activities. This process creates a multi-voiced system by which all individuals involved in the learning activity provide input on the activity design.

The LEARN Framework for Practice is not a Linear Process

Thus far, you've learned about *The Big Four* (L), examined *The Big Four* (E), and adopted/applied (A) a culturally meaningful framework. You also learned tools to guide you through reflecting (R) on your designed activities and negotiating (N) activities throughout this process. It is essential to know that *The LEARN Framework for Practice* is not linear. After you learn *The Big Four* and understand how to apply a framework when designing activities, you can move fluidly through the framework.

From this perspective, you may think of a need—such as a classroom community—and then share this need with students in which you negotiate the CHAT elements I discussed earlier. You may then adopt a framework to guide your practices on culturally meaningful teaching. When you adopt your framework, you may realize there are things you still need to learn (L) about your students to design culturally meaningful activities.

This is one example of how the framework is not linear; use it based on your needs rather than in the order I presented in this book. I believe, however, that it is best practice to follow *LEA*—learn, examine, adopt/apply—of the *LEARN* to gain foundational knowledge of culturally meaningful teaching. Over time, if you continue to use *The LEARN Framework* as a regular part of your practice, you will move back and forth with the framework with ease.

Allow the framework to be a sign for you. As street signs guide us within our communities, *The LEARN Framework for Practice* can guide you through designing culturally meaningful practices. From this perspective, *L* points to learning; the goal is to learn as much as possible regarding *The Big Four* and anything else you will need to learn about yourself, your students, and culturally meaningful teaching to design effective practices. The letter *E* points to examine; the goal is to examine *The Big Four*.

The letter *A* points to the need to adopt and apply a culturally meaningful framework when designing culturally meaningful practices. The goal is to follow culturally meaningful principles when designing activities. The letter *R* points to reflection; the goal is to reflect on your designed activity to determine if you achieved your goal and how you can enhance your design. The letter *N* points to negotiation; the goal is to negotiate all elements of the activity system—tools, object, community, rules, division of labor—with students to design effective activities that place the cultural values, community practices, and lived experiences of students at the center of instruction. Throughout this book, I argue that designing culturally meaningful practices requires specific tools. *The LEARN Framework for Practice* is a tool made for and by educators designed to guide school-based practitioners through unpacking culturally meaningful teaching and developing culturally meaningful practices.

Summary

In this chapter, I introduced the letter N of *The LEARN Framework*, which stands for negotiation. I described two ways you can negotiate your curriculum. I introduced the CHAT framework and described how you can negotiate tools, objects, rules, community, and division of labor when designing your activity.

What's Next?

Now that you have learned about the framework elements, you must do two things: (1) apply *The LEARN Framework for Practice* so you can co-design culturally meaningful activities with your students and (2) maintain the knowledge you've gained in this book so you will develop as a culturally competent educator. In the next chapter, I wrap things up by providing five maintenance tips so you can stay on the cutting edge of culturally meaningful teaching.

Cooling Down:
Maintaining Your Benefits

The real people who hold our civilization together are the maintenance people. If it weren't for them - pumping water out of subways, painting bridges to keep from rusting, fixing a steam pipe that is 70 years old - we'd be sunk. If we got rid of all the politicians and the policymakers in the world, the world would keep going. If you get rid of maintenance people, the whole thing breaks down.

—**Alan Weisman**

Chapter 14:

Maintenance

———————— ✖ ————————

> In order to design culturally responsive SEL activities, my needs remain the same as those of designing culturally responsive activities in general: instruction, application, reflection/discussion, and collaboration with others throughout the process.
>
> **—PhD Research Participant**

Have you ever made gains or progress in achieving some goal but then, over time, lost those gains and regressed to square one? Has this ever happened to you? I can think of a few instances in which this has happened. The first example that comes to mind is working out, in which I set specific goals regarding my health. I typically meet those goals, but over time, because of the business of life, I often regress to square one, and I lose the gains I had obtained and must start from scratch.

The second example that comes to mind is losing information. I have experienced making progress with learning new concepts and applying principles in the classroom. However, over time, I forgot the principles I applied in practice. I lost the knowledge because after I learned it, I did not rehearse it and apply the principles daily. This happens to the best of us, right? For learning, if we don't use it—or at least rehearse specific knowledge we learn—we will lose it.

In this chapter, I share five maintenance activities you can engage with, so you don't lose the information you learned from this book—so you don't regress to where you were before learning *The LEARN Framework* principles. By the end of this chapter, you will be able to:

- engage in five practical activities to maintain the benefits of this book;
- engage in activities to "internalize" *The LEARN Framework*, memorizing its five elements and applying them as a daily practice; and
- explain the benefits of joining a community of learners to maintain the benefits you gained from this book.

If you rehearse the maintenance tips for the next 90 days, I am confident you will maintain the knowledge you have gained from this book and internalize *The LEARN Framework for Practice*. In other words, from interacting with the framework consistently in practice, you will memorize and internalize *The Big Four*. That is, you will naturally employ principles from *The LEARN Framework*, and you won't need the *Culturally Meaningful Comparison Table* (see Chapters 15 and 16) to design culturally meaningful practices.

You will develop a justice-oriented mindset and naturally apply culturally meaningful principles as tools to achieve equity in the classroom. From internalizing the work, you go from providing "culturally responsive teaching" to simply "good teaching." You become inclusive. You make culturally responsive teaching a component of quality instruction. You also understand you cannot have quality instruction without culturally meaningful practices (Williams, 2015). Culturally meaningful teaching is the *engine* to quality instruction.

From internalizing this process, you may be able to design and re-design without having physical copies of frameworks next to you. Culturally meaningful teaching is a mindset, and it requires that you internalize culturally meaningful principles such that they become a part of your everyday practice. I call this *The Internalization Process*, internalizing culturally meaningful ways of thinking and being as an educator, based on culturally meaningful principles. In what follows, I share tips and opportunities for you so you can build upon your knowledge and not regress to where you were before reading this book. I share ideas on how you can internalize *The LEARN Framework* and make it a part of your everyday practice!

Five Maintenance Activities

One of my professors who taught qualitative research at the University of Illinois at Chicago (UIC) often said, "When you experience problems in your research design, if you ever become confused, if you feel that you want to give up, if you start crying—go back to your research questions." Jokingly, he illustrated that if researchers get stuck when conducting qualitative research, they should return to their research questions and then figure things out from there. Returning to the research question allows researchers to revisit the questions that inspired their study. It is a process of retracing their steps, revisiting the purpose for conducting their study.

As my professor encouraged us to return to the research questions that motivated our research when we experienced problems, I encourage you to return to *The LEARN Framework* when you experience problems that prevent you from designing culturally meaningful practices. Specifically, I encourage you to:

1. re-read *The Big Four* (**L**);
2. re-examine *The Big Four* (**E**);
3. select a framework, study it, and apply the framework principles in the classroom (**A**);
4. reflect on whether your designed practices are meeting the cultural needs of students (**R**); and

5. negotiate the curriculum by which you and your students co-plan, co-design, and co-lead activities during instructional time (**N**).

The goal of the above five maintenance activities is to maintain this book's benefits, including knowledge related to culturally meaningful teaching and how to design culturally meaningful practices. Since this is your first time learning about *The LEARN Framework*, you must re-read each element of the framework, starting with *The Big Four (L)*. Instead of reading or skimming *The Big Four*, read at a slower rate. Use the margins in the book as tools and jot down questions and insights that emerge from the reading.

There is no need to look for other resources to supplement this book. I recommend learning *The LEARN Framework* principles first before searching for additional resources. Once you internalize these principles, explore other principles, concepts, and perspectives on culturally responsive teaching. But learn *The LEARN Framework* principles first. I say this because the principles that comprise the framework are grounded in the history of culturally responsive education (CRE) scholarship. When you internalize *The LEARN Framework*, you:

- know your why;
- have solid knowledge of culturally responsive teaching and its history;
- can define and describe cultural values and community practices; and
- can apply frameworks in the classroom and use them as guides when designing culturally meaningful activities.

Once you get the *LEARN* principles down, start reading other resources on the topic. But get the *LEARN* principles down first before searching for other resources to supplement your learning. The reason you want to get *The LEARN Framework* down first is that it includes *The Big Four*; this is everything you need to know now to start re-imagining your practices and designing culturally meaningful activities immediately.

The Big Four is your foundation. You cannot design *intentionally* and *purposefully* without knowing it. Once you internalize *The LEARN Framework*, you'll be prepared to easily pair the principles with supplemental books, other theories, and classroom practices. Therefore, get the basics down first. That is, make sure you internalize *The Big Four* before printing additional articles and buying other books on the topic that might confuse you.

Private Facebook Community of Practice

During my dissertation defense, when I described the learning experiences of teachers and administrators in my study, I talked about the impact educators had on each other's learning. School-based practitioners not only learned from each other in the study, but they taught each other as they became familiar with useful tools, including frameworks. Practitioners within the study became a learning community. We learn much more within learning communities than in isolation from other knowledgeable peers, and here is why. When we learn within learning communities, we become resources for each other. We become a community of resources, and we can tap into each other's resources, try new tools and ideas, and use the new resources in the design process.

I encourage you to join *Redesign* private Facebook group so you can maintain the benefits gained from this book by processing the content with a community of educators. As a member of this group, you will have access to:

- free resources related to designing culturally meaningful activities;
- a community of educators developing culturally meaningful practices across content areas; and
- videos that further explain *The Big Four*—and more.

One of the greatest benefits of joining the private group is learning from other educators, including learning about the tools they are using to design culturally meaningful practices, learning about the challenges they have experienced and how they resolved them, and learning how students are responding to the designed activities, which is what I am always most excited about hearing. You can ask questions about the framework and get community support as you unpack culturally meaningful teaching and design culturally meaningful practices.

I will also host live question-and-answer sessions in the private group and create opportunities for peer-to-peer coaching related to academic content areas and social and emotional learning. The private community will create opportunities for teachers across grade levels to learn strategies specific to their areas of work. I designed the Facebook group to offer additional maintenance activities for you to access now that you have completed this book.

Peer coaching within this group will come from educators like you who have read this book and are now applying the principles in the classroom across subject areas with success. During my PhD research study, practitioners commented that, prior to the study, they had never seen examples of culturally responsive teaching in action and had no models to follow as guides to design culturally responsive activities. Major benefits of the private Facebook group are hearing stories from other teachers who are experiencing success with the framework and seeing culturally responsive teaching in action, from recorded videos and live training sessions by educators like you.

The LEARN Academy

If you want to take a deeper dive into the content of this book and access direct coaching from me, you may enroll in *The LEARN Academy*, an online training school dedicated to helping stakeholders like you unpack culturally meaningful teaching and design culturally meaningful practices using the 5-step *LEARN* framework.

During my 7-week PhD research study, practitioners commented that, although they had read popular books on culturally responsive teaching and attended hours of training on the topic, they had never learned how to design culturally responsive practices from scratch or how to re-imagine, adapt, or re-design their current practices in culturally meaningful ways. Sadly, their teacher training programs did not train them on culturally responsive teaching principles or design concepts. Their first time learning about culturally meaningful frameworks was during the PhD research study. After discussing this, I shared with one practitioner who participated in the study that we have all been duped! Training programs have trained us from Eurocentric lenses and ignored the cultural values, lived experiences, and community practices of culturally diverse learners. As a result, we now struggle to design culturally responsive practices.

I designed *The LEARN Academy* for individuals who desire to become competent at designing culturally meaningful practices. *The Academy* offers a host of classes that cover best practices in designing culturally meaningful activities from start to finish. *The Academy* includes courses related to using *The LEARN Framework* to design educational programming in culturally meaningful ways, including:

- community building activities across subject areas;
- multi-tiered system of supports (MTSS);
- transformative and culturally responsive SEL across tiers;
- trauma-informed supports;
- restorative justice practices;
- special education supports, 504 accommodations—and more!

In *The Academy*, I reveal the design and re-design principles I used in my PhD research study to help you unpack culturally meaningful frameworks and design culturally meaningful practices in a step-by-step fashion. In addition to learning how to apply *The LEARN Framework* with specific educational practices in your daily work at the ground level, you will learn how to:

- construct "design maps" to iterate with students;
- adapt pre-packaged, pre-planned, and prescriptive traditional curricula in culturally meaningful ways;
- analyze and problematize current practices, then redesign them in culturally meaningful ways; and
- iterate activities using four essential design principles.

In addition to these benefits, I will teach you the *3-Step Problem Transformation Process* (PTP) that emerged from my research study, consisting of *identifying, exploring,* and *transforming* problems to design effective, culturally meaningful practices. The *3-Step Transformation Process* is foundational to the design process. It starts with identifying problems that prevent you from developing culturally meaningful practices, exploring problems you can transform in a short amount of time, and employing specific tools you can use to transform those problems. This is the basic principle of mediation I discussed in Chapter 1, and in *The Academy,* I simplify this process and show you how to use it throughout the design process.

To provide equitable practices in the classroom, we must learn how to design using culturally meaningful principles, which I teach you how to do in the course. I believe, to achieve educational equity, it is critical that we learn how to design because prepackaged, pre-planned, and prescriptive curricula and lesson plans may not relate to our students' cultural values, interests, and lived experiences. Such programs may be insensitive to their experiences. If we lack knowledge of culturally meaningful practices, we will not know how to spot insensitive practices in the classroom, and we won't know how to adapt and redesign curricula in culturally meaningful ways based on our students' cultures and racial and cultural identities.

My final recommendations to you as I conclude this book include the following:

- keep your why at the forefront of your practice—reflect on it daily;
- expect to iterate activities because your designs may not be sufficient upon your first few attempts; and
- when you experience problems, feel doubtful, or feel you want to abandon the work—return to *The LEARN Framework*, join the private Facebook community group, and access *The LEARN Academy* to receive explicit, direct coaching on designing culturally meaningful activities.

Congratulations! I am confident that you are more equipped to design culturally meaningful practices now than before reading this book. Not only did you achieve agency in enhancing your knowledge of culturally meaningful teaching, but you also learned four tools you can use as guides when designing culturally meaningful activities. You learned about, processed, and examined *The Big Four;* you learned about three culturally meaningful frameworks you can draw from to guide you through the design process; you understand the importance of reflecting on and negotiating designed practices—and you have the tools to do it all in your classroom!

If we don't use what we learn, we will lose what we learn. In writing this book, I have used what I have learned. I shared insights I learned from my PhD study, including framework principles. I pulled together what I have learned over the past 12 years as a school-based practitioner and equity coach, and I placed it in this book so you can use it to enhance your knowledge and practice.

Now it is your turn to use what you have learned from this book to design culturally meaningful and equitable practices in the classroom. Take it one step at a time. Expect failure. Accept failure. Contact me when you need additional support.

I can't wait to hear about your learning experiences and success with employing *The LEARN Framework for Practice*. Meet your colleagues in the private Facebook group to continue this conversation and enroll in *The LEARN Academy*, so I can take you on a deeper dive in designing culturally meaningful practices and coach you on four essential design principles! I look forward to learning with you.

In solidarity,

Dwayne D. Williams, PhD

References

Alim, H. S., & Haupt, A. (2017). Reviving Soul (s) with afrikaaps. Culturally Sustaining Pedagogies: Teaching and Learning for Justice in a Changing World, 157.

Allen, B. A., & Boykin, A. W. (1992). African-American children and the educational process: Alleviating cultural discontinuity through prescriptive pedagogy. School Psychology Review, 21(4), 586-596.

Belgrave, F. Z., & Allison, K. W. (2014). Psychosocial adaptation and mental health. African American Psychology: From Africa to America, 409-44.

Biesta, G., & Tedder, M. (2007). Agency and learning in the lifecourse: Towards an ecological perspective. Studies in the Education of Adults, 39(2), 132-149.

Boykin, A. W., & Noguera, P. (2011). Creating the opportunity to learn: Moving from research to practice to close the achievement gap. Ascd.

Boykin, A. W., Tyler, K. M., & Miller, O. (2005). In search of cultural themes and their expressions in the dynamics of classroom life. Urban Education, 40(5), 521-549.

Jamison, D. (2014). Daudi Azibo: defining and developing Africana psychological theory, research and practice. Journal of Pan African Studies, 7(5).

Gay, G. (2014). Culturally responsive teaching principles, practices, and effects. Handbook of urban education, 1(1), 353-372.

Gay, G. (2018). Culturally responsive teaching: Theory, research, and practice. Teachers College Press.

Ladson-Billings, G. (1995). But that's just good teaching! The case for culturally relevant pedagogy. Theory into practice, 34(3), 159-165.

Mahfouz, J., & Anthony-Stevens, V. (2020). Why Trouble SEL? The Need for Cultural Relevance in SEL. Occasional Paper Series, 2020(43), 6.

Parham, T. A., Ajamu, A., & White, J. L. (2015). Psychology of Blacks: Centering our perspectives in the African consciousness. Psychology Press.

Paris, D. (2012). Culturally sustaining pedagogy: A needed change in stance, terminology, and practice. Educational researcher, 41(3), 93-97.

Seidel, S., Simmons, T., & Lipset, M. (2022). Hip-Hop Genius 2.0: Remixing High School Education. Rowman & Littlefield.

White, J. L., & Parham, T. A. (1990). The psychology of blacks (Second ed.). Englewood Cliffs, NJ: Prentice Hall.

Williams, D. D. (2015). An RTI guide to improving the performance of African American students. Corwin Press.

Williams, D.D. (2020). Redesign: An sel toolkit to designing culturally sustaining and antiracist practices. Being With Their Culture.

Appendix

Useful Tools for Designing Culturally Meaningful Activities

During my PhD research study, practitioners commented that they could not design culturally responsive practices because they needed more tools. The tools practitioners acquired from their training programs and implemented in the classroom centered on Eurocentric norms and ignored the lived experiences, community practices, and cultural values of culturally diverse learners. In addition, practitioners had never been trained in culturally responsive frameworks, so they needed to learn how to use culturally meaningful principles to guide their designs. By the end of the study, however, practitioners and I co-designed tools to transform their problems; then, we used co-designed tools to develop culturally meaningful activities.

In what follows, I include a list of resources practitioners found useful for unpacking culturally responsive teaching and designing culturally responsive practices. Since the purpose of this section is to give you these resources and keep the section short, I will not describe each tool in detail. Instead, I have created videos and placed them in our *Redesign* private Facebook group. In that group, we explore tools, and I explain how to use them to critique current practices. We use them to redesign activities in culturally meaningful ways.

Appendix A

Useful Tools for Unpacking Culturally Responsive Teaching and Designing Culturally Meaningful Activities

Practitioners identified the following 14 tools as useful for unpacking culturally responsive teaching and designing culturally responsive practices. Tools are listed in alphabetical order rather than by usefulness:

1. articles
2. calendar
3. CHAT framework
4. coaching
5. concrete examples
6. culturally meaningful frameworks
7. deficit-asset comparison table
8. discussions with colleagues
9. examples
10. *Funds of Knowledge* survey
11. hands on activities
12. homework
13. PowerPoint content on the history of culturally responsive education
14. storytelling

Of the 14 resources, practitioners identified the following *four* as the most helpful for unpacking culturally responsive teaching and designing culturally responsive activities.

1. articles
2. CHAT framework
3. *Culturally Meaningful Comparison Table*
4. *Funds of Knowledge* Survey

Join us in our *Redesign* private Facebook group to learn more about these resources.

1. Article

The most helpful reading resource was the magazine *Demystifying Culturally Responsive Teaching: In The Beginning was . . . Racism.* You can download this magazine for free at our website: www.tier1education.com. Practitioners commented that this resource was effective in helping them understand the history of culturally responsive education. They stated that understanding the history grounded them in the work and gave them their *why*. Subscribe to our newsletter to access this magazine and other free booklets and resources.

2. CHAT Framework

Instead of piling quick-tip, technical solutions on top of old, outdated resources, we critiqued current practices to identify cultural clashes that present in the classroom. We analyzed our current practices/lessons from a critical lens. Here is the visual we used to do it:

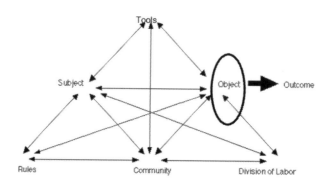

Please see Chapter 12 for a review of the CHAT framework and its elements. We provide examples in the *Redesign* private Facebook group on how to use the CHAT framework as an *analytical tool* to critique and problematize our practices. We use this tool to identify cultural clashes in the classroom. We then use this tool as a *design template* to re-imagine our practices in culturally meaningful ways.

3. Culturally Meaningful Comparison Table

At the start of the training, practitioners were unfamiliar with culturally responsive frameworks. Consequently, they could not design culturally responsive practices intentionally and purposefully, using culturally responsive principles in meaningful ways. They identified *The Culturally Meaningful Comparison Table* as the most helpful tool compared to all other resources. In their words:

> Lack of knowledge was my initial concern along with not having a lot of time to focus on [culturally responsive teaching]. As the study continued, my concerns evolved to "how do I apply this [culturally responsive principles] to each situation?" I then decided to just focus on the table [*The Culturally Meaningful Comparison Table*] and use that to guide me through each situation.
>
> **—PhD Research Participant**

> It was really helpful to have the table [*Culturally Meaningful Comparison Table*] that included the prominent scholar, definition, guiding principles, and prominent article. I was able to use that to guide me in everything that I did. The only problem is that I still need the table.
>
> **—PhD Research Participant**

Culturally Meaningful Comparison Table

Frameworks:	Culturally *Relevant* Pedagogy	Culturally *Responsive* Teaching	Culturally *Sustaining* Pedagogy
Scholar:	Gloria Ladson-Billings	Geneva Gay	Django Paris
Definitions:	"A pedagogy of opposition, not unlike critical pedagogy, but specifically committed to collective, not merely individual empowerment" (Ladson-Billings, 1995, p. 160).	"Culturally responsive teaching uses the cultural orientations, heritages, and background experiences of students of color as referents and resources to improve their school achievement" (Gay, 2014, p. 357).	A pedagogy that "seeks to perpetuate and foster—to sustain—linguistic, literate, and cultural pluralism as part of the democratic project of schooling" (Paris, 2012, p. 93).
Guiding Principles:	1. Students will experience academic success. 2. Students will develop/maintain cultural competence and academic excellence. 3. Students will develop a critical consciousness through which they challenge the status quo and current social order (Ladson-Billings, 1995. pp. 160-161).	1. A need to teach to and through students. 2. A need to build bridges for teachers and students to cross. 3. Race, ethnicity, and culture matter profoundly in teaching and learning. 4. Changing perceptions of underachieving students from problems to possibilities (Gay, 2014, pp. 357-359).	1. A focus on the plural and evolving nature of **youth identity** and **cultural practices** and a commitment to embracing youth culture's counter-hegemonic potential; 2. While maintaining a clear-eyed critique of how youth culture can also reproduce systemic inequalities (Paris & Alim, 2014, p. 85).
Prominent Article:	Ladson-Billings, G. (1995). But that's just good teaching! The case for culturally relevant pedagogy.	Gay, G. (2014). Preparing for culturally responsive teaching.	Paris, D. (2012). Culturally sustaining pedagogy: A needed change in stance, terminology, and practice.

4. Funds of Knowledge Survey

While reading the magazine *Demystifying Culturally Responsive Teaching,* practitioners learned about Ladson-Billings's (1995), Gay's (2014), and Paris's (2012) frameworks. They discovered that a core component of culturally responsive teaching is centering the lived experiences, cultural values, and community practices of culturally diverse learners in the classroom. However, they had no idea how to gather this information from students.

Based on this obstacle, I designed a survey that practitioners could use to collect information about their students' cultural interests, community practices, and lived experiences. Practitioners then adapted the survey to meet their needs. Following is the original survey I designed. I presented the survey to practitioners during the training; they adapted it—i.e., included information based on their needs—and used it to gather data on their students' cultural interests and values. They then used the data they gathered to co-design community-building activities with students.

Questions:	Responses:
Categories of music I listen to:	
Artists I listen to within those categories:	
My favorite TV shows/movies are:	
My hobbies are:	

My gifts and talents include: (rapping, singing, poetry, drawing, dancing, presenting, photography, writing, creating relationships, and/or others), other: Include others if not listed	
Things my family and I do during family gatherings/family reunions:	
Things that have been happening in society that I think about and want to talk about:	
My favorite subjects are:	
My least favorite subjects are:	
Adults that I have relationships with in the building:	

Join us in our *Redesign* Facebook group to learn more about how we used this survey to identify our students' cultural values, community practices, and lived experiences. Join us and dive deeper into how to use these four resources to design culturally meaningful practices and how to create goals and objectives using principles from a variety of culturally meaningful frameworks.

Made in the USA
Las Vegas, NV
05 July 2023

74252233R00133